How to grow and use
HERBS ON YOUR WINDOWSILL, BALCONY OR PATIO

How to grow and use

HERBS ON YOUR WINDOWSILL, BALCONY OR PATIO

Anne Chamberlain

GUILD PUBLISHING
LONDON

This edition published 1985
by Book Club Associates
by arrangement with
W. Foulsham & Company Limited,
Yeovil Road, Slough, Berkshire SL1 4JH

Photoset in Great Britain by Input Typesetting Ltd,
London SW19

Printed in Spain by Cayfosa. Barcelona
Dep. leg. B - 7891-1985

CONTENTS

THE STORY OF HERBS

The story of herbs is nearly as ancient as that of Man. Aromatic plants have been part of man's existence since the earliest years, with their medicinal and preservative properties and delicate flavours. The ancient Egyptians showed an appreciation of aromatic herbs (bunches of herbs have been found in mummies' hands) and they were widely used in Ancient Greece and Rome. The Hebrews and Mohameddans used herbs as part of their religion, and they are mentioned in both the Bible and the Koran.

All ancient medicine was herbal, and the father of medicine, Hippocrates, used four hundred herbs in his Temple of Aesculapius in Greece in the fourth century B.C. The Hippocratic Oath is still taken by doctors, and some two hundred of Hippocrates' original herbs are still used medically. It is important to remember that these are not necessarily herbs as we know them, as the word *herbage* was originally applied to any kind of plant, and tree fruits, leaves, bulbs and flowers were used.

British herbal history began with the Romans when an Army doctor called Dioscorides prepared his *Materia Medica* in 100 A.D., which was used as the basis of medical practice for sixteen centuries. The Romans introduced Parsley, Rue, Onion, Fennel, Rosemary, Sage and Thyme to Britain. In 1066, that famous historical date, the first English herbal was written, based on the teachings of Apuleius Platonicus, and this is now in the British Museum.

The cultivation of herbs flourished in the Middle Ages, mostly in the monasteries, manors and rectories. Not only were herbs used for medicine, but they were strewn on floors along with rushes to scent and purify the air. They were used to preserve food and improve flavours, often necessary in the days of trying to keep meat for long winter months. The upper classes appreciated the scent of herbs to keep out the overpowering smells of the lower orders, and this is commemorated in the nosegay or *tussie mussie* carried by judges to this day.

There are many strange beliefs connected with herbs, which could be dangerous. The Anglo-Saxon name for a medical herb was a 'wort' as in St. John's Wort, so many of the early healing plants can easily be identified. A German doctor called Paracelsus introduced a dangerous *Doctrine of Signatures* in the early sixteenth century which suggested that each plant was identified by its colour, scent or habit with the disease it cured, such as eyebright or lungwort, and this dangerous idea lingered on for centuries. Herbs were also identified with astrology, and people used the plants with due regard to the astrological signs under which they thrived. This practice was finally stamped out by Charles II when he founded the College of

Physicians and the Royal Society to regulate the practice of healing, just when herbal botany was at its peak.

Many towns such as Oxford, had their own botanical gardens, and their commercial herb gardens, particularly in the areas near London. Mitcham became famous for lavender and mint, but further afield, Pontefract specialised in liquorice and Banbury in rhubarb. There was a Physick Garden in Fetter Lane and a Herbal Garden at Kew, and the Chelsea Physick Garden which was founded by the Society of Apothecaries, still remains.

Many famous gardener/herbalists recorded their knowledge, which has come down to us. Gerard, who composed a great Herbal, was the Chairman of the Company of Barber Surgeons; Culpeper wrote a Physical Directory and gave his name to the Society of Herbalists; and Parkinson was appointed King's Herbalist to Charles I.

Culpeper's book was based on the connection between astrology and plants, and he felt they were cure-alls for every disease. Herbal medicine has a sound basis in fact, for many herbs have narcotic, digestive or cooling qualities, and many old wives' remedies are not as silly as they sound. Many people alive today were given concoctions of Rhubarb and Liquorice, or doses of Rue or Nettles, particularly in the spring, to purge winter evils and purify the blood.

Herb growing flourished in the houses and cottages of Elizabethan and Stuart times, when the housewife had to prepare her own simple medicines, and also her beauty aids and culinary herbs for preserving and flavouring. In 1573, agricultural writer Thomas Tusser recommended some twenty-one aromatic plants for strewing on floors to release their scent when trodden upon, including: Basil, Balm, Camomile, Costmary, Lavender, Hyssop, Sage and Thyme. Sir Hugh Plat, who wrote books for the country housewife on cooking, distilling and making beauty preparations, suggested in 1609 that in summer the large fireplace could be trimmed with a bank of fresh moss with a Rosemary pot at each end.

A visitor to England in 1560 noticed the pots of Rosemary and Lavender hung on the walls of our houses, and noticed, 'The neat cleanliness, the exquisite fineness, the pleasant and delightful furniture. . . the chambers and parlours strewed over with sweet herbs!'

At the accession of James II, a Strewer of Herbs in Ordinary to His Majesty was appointed, and as late as the Coronation of George IV there was a Herb Strewer. Servants were employed to fumigate the rooms of large houses, and professional perfumers were sometimes called to travel to perform the same function. Scented herbs were burned on large fires, and no room was complete without its bowl of pot pourri, usually made by the lady of the house, however grand she might be. This use of scented herbs was so much part of people's lives that it was commented on frequently by Shakespeare and Bacon and by many early cookery and gardening writers, and no home was considered worthy of the name without its little plot of herbs and its stillroom in which scented concoctions were prepared.

Sadly, the growing and use of herbs began to decline during the nineteenth century when many wild herbs were found growing extensively in Europe and more organised cultivation, collection and distribution became possible as machines and transport improved. The USA with its variety of soil and climate became the ideal place to grow vast quantities of drug herbs and there was little need for domestic herb gardens to be cultivated. The Victorians only used some forty herbs instead of the earlier hundreds, and now we only use perhaps half a dozen regularly.

During the 1914–18 War, herb growing revived with the Voluntary Herb Growers Association, but there was no financial aid and once again the craft declined, although herb-growing continued to flourish in France, Germany and Italy which built up large drug and perfumery industries.

Yet another revival was staged in the emergency of the 1939–45 War with a National Herb Organiser and Country Herb Committees cultivating plants for medical purposes as well as organising the collection of nettles, rose hips and chestnuts, some of which were used for making camouflage dyes.

Farmers are still encouraged to grow herbs for medical purposes, including Digitalis (foxglove) for heart medicines, Rosemary, Fennel, Opium Poppy and Henbane, but now the pendulum has swung again and many people are reviving the old and delightful arts of cultivating and using herbs as their Elizabethan ancestors did.

Those lucky enough to have a little land can plan out old-fashioned square gardens or borders for herbs, with perhaps a few roses interspersed. Many herbs have the great advantage of being mainly evergreen and make beautiful plants which are easy to care for throughout the year, and give pleasure throughout the seasons. Even without a garden, we can return to the old-style tubs, pots and hanging gardens of our ancestors, and enjoy again the delicious scents and fragrant flavours of home-grown herbs.

HOW AND WHERE TO GROW HERBS

Growing herbs in a small space is not difficult or expensive. Little equipment is needed, nor extensive gardening knowledge. Try a few everyday herbs first, and you will soon find yourself enjoying experiments in growing and using more exotic varieties.

BASIC GARDENING EQUIPMENT

A small trowel and fork, intended in the first place for the use of children in the garden, make very handy tools for container work. Sometimes these are sold for house plant maintenance. The trowel is small enough to use for transplanting seedlings without disturbing other plants, and the fork is useful for breaking up the top soil, which may be necessary occasionally.

Weeds should not present too great a problem in containers if sterilised growing composts are used. These compounds, made up of all the basic nutrients that plants will need at all stages of growth, can be bought in bags of various sizes from most stores and garden shops. John Innes seed-sowing compost is the most useful, and seeds can be sown in this before transferring them into pots of John Innes No 1 potting compost when the seedlings are large enough to handle. John Innes No 2 or 3 is suitable for the large containers into which growing plants will be finally transplanted.

Do not let the compost or soil mixtures cause you to worry, as growing plants are adept at taking just what nutrients they require, and no more, from the medium in which they are being grown.

A small, light watering can with a long spout and fine rose is also useful for easy regular watering, together with a supply of plant labels and a few spare flower pots.

SOWING SEED

The kitchen, which is usually the warmest room, can be used as a nursery for experimenting and growing some of the lesser-known herbs from seed. Although small flowerpots can be used for seed growing providing only a small pinch of seed is sown, a very useful little propagator can be bought which consists of a small plastic tray and a clear plastic hood which covers the seed tray. This small propagator, if filled with John Innes seed compost, will hold four or five different varieties of herbs, if a small line only of each is sown. The plants can be transferred to larger containers when they are large enough to handle and spare plants can be potted into fancy flowerpots as gifts. Pot Marjoram for instance, or the Dwarf White Lavender make most fragrant and pretty pot plants. A few labels on which to write the name of the individual herbs will also be required.

Some herb seeds can be extremely slow germinating. While lavender will only take fourteen to eighteen days to germinate, Sweet Marjoram needs up to seventy days so allow plenty of time for seeds to make an appearance.

CUTTINGS

It may be necessary to take cuttings from time to time from growing plants so that stock of a favourite bush or shrub can be increased. Cuttings of new growths taken from a shrub can be planted around the edge of a flowerpot and covered with a plastic bag until established. Another method is to purchase a small plastic bag containing a root compound, which can be bought ready-filled. Holes need to be cut in the flat side of the bag, into which cuttings are inserted, after watering well. Keep the bag in the warm, away from drying winds and hot sunlight, until the cuttings have rooted and are growing well. They can then be individually transplated into small flowerpots, and spare ones would make delightful gifts for friends.

Year-Round Maintenance

All flower pots and containers with herbs in them, which are situated in the house behind a window, or in the open air on balconies, will need to be turned, in some instances twice a week, so that each side of the growing plant has the opportunity to receive some sunlight. This applies to a lesser degree to herbs which may be growing in small tubs in very shady corners in a courtyard or on a patio. If the containers are turned when the taller herbs lean towards the light, the plant will then straighten and maintain a uniformity of growth.

Although odd leaves may be taken from the growing plants to use for flavouring at any stage of the growth of the herb, the main harvesting of leaves for preservation should be just before the plants bloom.

If the beauty of the flowers is important in a herb garden, the stems and leaves can be cut after the flowers blossom and fade, although there may be a slight deterioration in the strength of the flavour of the dried herb. In a good summer another growth of stems is available for cutting and storing, after the first main harvesting, especially during September. When cutting the stems for drying or freezing, try not to mutilate the plant but leave a little stem and a few leaves growing from the soil, if possible, to encourage the plant to grow on for a little longer. The Mints will tolerate hard cutting, but shrub plants like Sage should be left neatly trimmed and tidy.

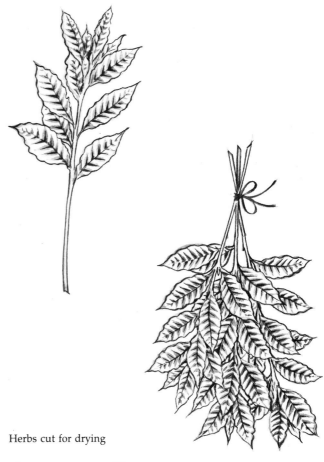

Herbs cut for drying

Annuals, Perennials and Biennials

In many seed catalogues and gardening books, the terms *annual*, *perennial* and *biennial* are often used to indicate the way a plant grows and can be propagated. These terms can greatly influence herb gardening if one wants to rely on having a supply of favourite herbs either fresh or dried.

Annual (including Half Hardy Annual)

This is a plant whose seed is sown in the spring. This can be February or March for indoor growing. The seeds can be sown in a small flower pot or a small propagator. The seeds of annuals must be sown very, very thinly in the pot and covered lightly with a sprinkling of seed-growing compost. The pot can be enclosed in a plastic bag, after being well-watered, until the seeds have germinated.

As soon as germination takes place, the bag should be removed from the pots or the plastic hood should be taken off a propagator so that the seedlings can strengthen. When the seedlings are growing strongly, they should be thinned by pulling out the weaker plants (water the plants before attempting this), leaving in the pot just the amount of plants required for containers. The seedlings can then be hardened off gradually by putting them out on a balcony or standing them in a windowbox during the daylight hours, and bringing them indoors again at night, until all danger of night frost is past, usually towards the end of May.

Transfer the seedlings to outdoor containers during the end of this month and they will be ready for drying and preserving at the end of July, August and September. They take roughly two or three months to mature fully, depending on weather conditions, although the odd leaf or two can be picked when required during the growing stage. If a particular annual grows a little taller than anticipated and smothers other herbs growing in the same container, use a few twigs from a hedge to insert around the offending plant until harvest time. These will give the taller plants some support. The annuals are inclined to be more frail and straggly than perennials and rich soil in the container may encourage this fault, but the additional support will stop them dominating the container in which they are growing.

Hardy Annuals

These can be cultivated in the same way as the annuals, but they will also tolerate early spring weather changes, so if space in the nursery is limited, the seeds of hardy annuals can be sown directly into large containers where they are to mature. The seedlings will have to be thinned as before and the thinnings can be transferred into other containers and tubs if required.

Perennials

Perennial herbs may also be raised from seed, although a great deal of patience is required from the gardener. Seed can be sown either in the spring or autumn months in a not-too-rich compost if strong sturdy plants are wanted. Seed must be sown thinly, otherwise small spindly seedlings will be the result. The propagator hood or the plastic bag covering the container in which the seed is sown must be taken off as soon as the seedlings have germinated and are showing above the compost. The seedlings need to be in a warm but shady situation at this stage until they are about 5 cm/2 in high, when they can be transplated into individual pots. the plants need to be handled very carefully when being transplanted. The coffee cups used in vending machines, or yogurt and ice cream containers make handy little pots for the transplanted seedlings. Remember to make a small hole in the bottom of the pots to assist drainage. Once the seedlings are established and seem to be growing well, they can be placed on a sunny part of the balcony or patio, providing they are watered as necessary. The aim is to have a strong sturdy plant ready to face the winter months. During the winter, the top growth will die down and can be trimmed off. The plant will remain dormant but should be stood in a sheltered spot on a balcony or patio away from prevailing winds and the worst of the weather. If the weather is too hard and cold, the plants can be enclosed in plastic bags. Growth should start again in the following spring and the plants can then be placed in more permanent positions. Considering the time required from seed sowing to full maturity (practically two years) one can understand why patience is required.

A much quicker and easier way of increasing the stock of a favourite herb is by taking cuttings. A root of the herb will have to be bought in the first instance, and during the spring or early summer months cuttings can be taken from the parent plant and inserted either in a flower pot containing John Innes compost or in a rooting compound.

Taking a cutting from Rosemary

Dipping the heel in rooting compost

Cuttings are generally new growths which can be seen growing between the leaf axils. These need to be pulled carefully from the parent plant leaving what is termed a *heel* which includes a little of the old wood from the parent stock. The bottom leaves of the cutting need to be removed so that when the cutting is inserted, either around the edge of the spot or into the rooting compound, direct contact between the compost and the *heel* of the cutting is made. For this reason, be sure that the compost is well watered before inserting the cutting, and also that the new plant is firmly bedded into the growing medium. Keep the cuttings in the shade until growth is established, and water well, but not excessively or the new plants may dampen off and rot in the soil.

During late autumn or early spring, some perennial plants can be increased by division. This means digging out the perennial herb from its container and breaking off small pieces from the main rootstock. The divisions can be re-planted in new homes and, if this dividing of roots is carried out before the herb plants are making their spring growth, success in increasing stock in this manner can be practically guaranteed.

Try first experiments in root division on Mint or Chive roots, and first cuttings from Sage, to give some idea of increasing stock the cheapest way.

Biennials

This term merely means 'two years', which with some herbs is the length of time from sowing until the harvesting of the seed which is obtained from the bloom of the plant. Caraway,

Root division: Breaking off a piece from the main root stock

The divisions planted in a trough beside the parent plant

for instance, comes under this heading, and also nasturtium, if the seeds of this plant are required (nasturtium seeds are used green so the plant can also be called an annual). Correctly speaking, a biennial needs to be sown in the summer or autumn months of the year so that sturdy plants are obtained for lasting through the winter. The biennial will then move on quickly during the spring months and produce bloom and consequent seed for drying or reproduction the second year.

WINDOWSILL HERBS

Herbs are accommodating little plants and a useful assortment can be grown if a sunny window is the only space available. Of course, all growing plants like fresh air, so a kitchen window can always be opened on sunny days to give the plants a tonic. They, in turn, will produce their delightful fragrance and beautiful flowers.

An amateur who is not used to growing plants indoors may be best advised in the first instance to buy one root of each herb most used for cooking, from a nursery or garden centre. Roots of Mint, Sage and Thyme and even Parsley might be a good first selection. These little plants may well be growing in very small plastic pots and will have to be transferred into slightly larger flowers pots or other suitable containers, which will mean buying a small bag of growing compost. John Innes No 2 is suitable for this.

An old, but colourful, biscuit tin, with drainage holes knocked in the bottom, makes a useful plant-holder and the lid will fit nicely on the bottom of the tin to catch any water which filters through the compost during watering. To make sure that the drainage holes in the tin are kept free from clogging, break up an old saucer or cup and put the pieces in the bottom of the tin over the holes before putting in the compost. This will help to maintain the compost in good condition.

Growing bags

Another useful idea for a container which will sit very comfortably on an inside window ledge is a very small growing bag. The bags are filled with growing composts containing all the nutriments required for strong and healthy plants. The bag should be laid flat on its side, then holes can be cut on the uppermost side in which the herb roots are planted. Each bag will accommodate three or four plants comfortably. Watering needs to be attended to very carefully as it is easy to overwater this type of container, and many herbs prefer a warm soil, slightly on the dry side.

Herbs for windowsills

Keep any Mint in a separate pot or container on the window ledge, so that the roots do not spread and dominate all the growing area available. One or two Garlic cloves sown in a pot will grow happily on a window ledge and not present any problems, and a pot or two of Rosemary will provide fragrance and beautiful blooms. If a house has very large windows, a modern floor stand which holds four or five pots containing various herb plants looks most attractive in a living room. Cottage Geraniums look attractive in this, or the annual Sweet Marjoram.

Herbs on the windowsill in a variety of containers

For a good selection of herbs on the ledge inside the kitchen window, when no outside ledge is available, have a variety of containers. Try Parsley, Sage and Chives in a growing bag; Garlic in a pot; Sweet Marjoram or Burnet in a pot; Dwarf Lavender and perhaps Thyme in a tin; and Mint in a pot.

Although the pots and the tin will require watering daily during summer months, watering will have to be attended to more carefully for the growing bag. One watering every two or three days may be all that is required.

WINDOW BOXES

In a window box, a selection of growing herbs can be greater, and will be decorative as well as useful. A wooden window box painted on the outside only (so that no harmful fumes can interfere with the health of the growing plants) in a colour to match the paintwork of the house looks most attractive. The box can be as wide as the window and should be at least 30 cm/1 ft deep with drainage holes made in the bottom. These holes can then be covered with broken crocks before a growing medium is tipped in. Needless to say, somehow or other the box will have to be anchored securely to the window sill, either by fancy brackets or by staples inserted directly into the windowsill structure. For a ground floor flat, where the box's security is not so important, plastic troughs of various widths and depths can be purchased in many ornamental designs. Some also have their own drip tray. These troughs also look very attractive alongside a wide front porch, planted with the fragrant herbs which will give a warm welcome to any callers. Lavender, Rosemary, or Lemon Thyme might be good choices for this situation.

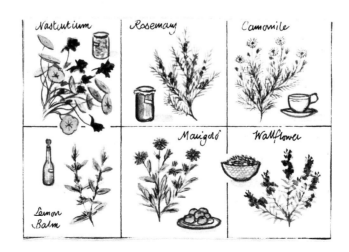

BALCONIES

A balcony, even if it is seventeen floors above street level in a tower block of flats is a wonderful asset for a herb grower in town. Although herbs will grow easily in such confined spaces especially on a balcony which receives plenty of sunshine for most of the day, the actual work of setting up such a garden can raise a few problems. It is difficult to bring a concrete or wooden tub to the required position on the balcony and a large amount of compost is needed to fill the tub. It is worth remembering that the balcony floor area may only receive direct sunlight for a few hours daily. It will be necessary to move around and re-position the various tubs and boxes so that the shade-loving plants such as Mint and Sage can be grown in the darker corners, leaving the sunnier spots for the other plants. Bearing this in mind, it may be advisable to start with the type of ornamental trough recommended for window boxes. These can be sited around the edge of a balcony leaving an area clear in the centre for working, repotting and any gardening job required. There may be room in a large balcony floor area to have one or two of the smaller troughs, with perhaps two small shrub tubs. Some have been made with a woodgrain effect and look most attractive in the corners of a balcony with the taller varieties of herbs growing in them.

On a balcony one looks down on to the plants, as it is not advisable to have boxes or hanging baskets suspended above the level of the safety rail, so the containers need not be visually attractive. Small plastic buckets in an assortment of bright colours can be just as decorative, as well as being easier to move around and arrange differently, giving greater scope for a bigger selection of herbs. Many plastic shrub tubs or troughs have no drainage holes and these holes will have to be punched in the bottom before putting in crocks and then filling up with compost. To assist drainage, and because it is a good idea to wash down the working area of the floor of the balcony occasionally, it is advisable to stand all troughs, tubs and buckets

on some sort of platform, so that all washing water can run freely beneath. Standing all containers on screw top lids from coffee or jam jars will allow enough clearance underneath the boxes for this purpose.

Another way of arranging plant troughs, especially on very small balconies where a small sitting room door opens out is to have one trough sitting on the lids on the concrete floor, with another trough immediately behind, raised on bricks placed at each corner of the trough. A third trough can be placed behind the second with two bricks at each corner. The bricks would have to be bought, of course, and would be another weight to hump up the stairs, but boxes placed like this do leave a small area for working on the balcony, which is so important for anyone living in a block of flats.

Hanging baskets are a great danger on balconies, as apart from the risk of continually knocking heads on them, there is always the possibility that they will fall to the street below on a windy day. All herbs should be confined to the floor of the balcony or at least below the level of the safety rail.

Garden equipment for balconies

With the main herbs growing on a balcony, all young seedlings can be grown indoors near the window of a kitchen or living room and transplanted outside when weather conditions permit. The walls surrounding most balconies usually give warmer conditions than experienced in outdoor gardens, and herbs may need watering twice a day during the hot summer months. After each watering, a can of cold water straight from the tap should be left on the balcony ready for the next watering. This water will become air-warmed and not be such a shock to the herbs which prefer a warm soil. This warm water will maintain the compost in better condition, and warmth will be retained.

Apart from a trowel, hand fork, plant labels and flower pots, a small watering can with a rose attachment will be required, so that an occasional overhead spray can be given to the plants, especially in the evening. This will freshen the leaves, although some balconies (depending on which way the wind is blowing) receive a little rain water just inside the safety rail, and each container in turn should be given the opportunity to receive some of this, if it is possible during a heavy rainstorm.

When the seedlings are large enough to handle for transplanting, put the pot containing the plants out on to the balcony during the day and bring them indoors at night, just for a few days to harden them off. They will not suffer any setback when finally moved to their permanent positions. Before planting into large containers, firm the top of the compost which should be ready waiting in the large pots for the new occupants. When transplanting, handle the seedlings carefully, make a small hole with a trowel in the compost and put the roots of the seedling in. Water with air-warmed water and then put a little compost around the roots and firmly bed in the plant. Water the plants well again with air-conditioned water, and if the weather is exceptionally warm and sunny, shade the plants for a few days with a sheet of paper, until they are established and growing well.

Although there is ample room for containers and tubs on a small balcony, these must remain on the floor of the balcony, but additional flower pots can be placed on the ledge *inside* the windows. This is a wonderful situation for the attractive and fragrant shrubs and plants. Their beauty and fragrance will be most noticeable after the evening watering, especially if an occasional overhead watering with a fine rose on a small watering can is given. Try Lemon Verbena, Sweet Marjoram, Camomile or one of the Thyme family, and the weather prophet, Burnet.

PATIOS AND VERANDAHS

Containers for growing herbs on patios and verandahs can cover a much wider and more interesting field. An old wheelbarrow, painted and filled with John Innes compost, gives ample room for a wide variety of shrubs and plants, although sun-lovers or those preferring shade should be grouped together if at all possible.

Although a great many decorative containers made in wood, fibreglass, plastic or concrete can be bought, ordinary household utensils no longer required for their original purpose can look most attractive with an assortment of the more colourful herbs growing in them. Old coal scuttles past their prime can be filled with bright marigolds. One or two cottage geraniums and nasturtiums creeping over the sides of the scuttles look good especially if they are standing on steps leading up to a verandah. On a small verandah, a grouped display of flowerpots filled perhaps with Lemon Thyme, Summer Savory, Eau de Cologne, Mint and Pot Marjoram can stand on a piece of pine wood laid across

the top of the treadle of an old sewing machine. Pots containing other herbs can be tied to the legs of the treadle, and the wrought-iron work makes a good background for the colourful blooms of the herbs and the various shades of green foliage.

Tall herbs for verandahs

Although a slightly larger container may be required for a Bay tree the base of the tree can always be used to grow other small growing herbs so the available space will not be wasted.

23

The walls surrounding patios and verandahs give shelter from the prevailing winds that a Bay tree appreciates. If the tree finally outgrows its home, it is so attractive that one can usually find a good home for it in a friend's garden after trying to propagate some cuttings, so that the new stock is available and will fit into smaller tubs.

Patios offer great possibilities for the growing of herbs if a small selection of the taller varieties such as Rosemary or Lavender can be grown in a shady corner directly in the soil. This can be done by lifting one or two of the paving stones normally used in this type of situation, and will lend more interest to the arrangement of herbs as well as blocking the appearance of a solid wall.

Window boxes can also be used, hanging from brackets drilled into the walls, or shelves can be made large enough to hold a collection of small flower pots or containers in which coloured herbs can be grown. As an alternative, a raised bed can easily be made, either across the corners of the patio or in a fancy shape, using bricks for the wall of the bed about 30 cm/1 ft high, and as far away from the boundary wall as needed. This can then be filled with a small layer of rubble or crocks before being topped up with a growing compost.

Sinks

The growing of plants in these movable containers makes this form of gardening much easier and more pleasurable for senior citizens or for people who find bending difficult. An old sink, for example, can be raised with two or three bricks at each corner to enable an older person or one confined to a wheelchair to grow herbs with some degree of comfort. The sink should be raised slightly higher at one corner so that water will flow directly to the waste water outlet, and the water outlet itself should be covered with broken pieces of crock so that there is never any blockage at this point. If additional crocks are laid across the bottom of the sink before finally filling with compost then the growing medium will always remain sweet smelling and pure for the growing plants. Different varieties of Thyme look attractive growing in the sink, especially if one or two large stones are laid on top of the compost and Pennyroyal is planted at the base so that this delightful herb can scramble over the stones. Colourful Sages also look attractive, growing in one corner of the sink.

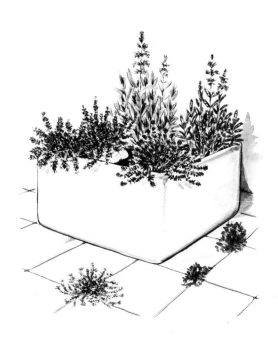

COURTYARDS

Many people in towns only have a miserable courtyard and the soil is too poor to allow much to grow. Courtyards are ideal places for experiment and improvement, and for making into

herb gardens. Fancy paving stones can be laid, leaving small gaps between the stones into which compost may be put down for planting creeping Thymes and Camomile. When these are walked on, they will release their delightful fragrance. Part of the courtyard can be raised on a slightly higher level and steps made to the raised part. Tubs may be situated each side of the steps, one containing a Bay tree and the other a selection of fragrant herbs. A boundary wall separating the two parts of the courtyard can be made with cavity-type breeze blocks, and the cavities filled with compost. Lemon Thyme, Burnet, and the Dwarf Lavenders look delightful growing in the cavities. The outer side of the breeze blocks may be whitened with limewash or emulsion paint to disguise their true identity. If one or two paving stones can be omitted in a convenient area, this small piece of soil can be improved sufficiently to grow one of the taller varieties of Rosemary, kept clipped to form a screening hedge behind which the dustbin can be kept out of view.

Hanging Baskets

Hanging baskets are ideal for growing herbs on patios, verandahs or in courtyards. They can be bought from most shops dealing with the sale of garden equipment. Traditionally made of galvanised wire, there are now baskets in plastic-covered wire in assorted colours. When planting a hanging basket, it is best to stand the basket on top of a large flower pot or bucket to keep it steady. To prevent soil or compost falling through the wire, line the basket with moss if possible. Sphagnum moss can usually be bought from garden shops, but plastic sheeting can be used, providing one or two holes are made in the bottom to assist drainage. A very attractive basket arrangement can be made by half-filling the basket with John Innes compost and then carefully pushing in the roots of growing plants through the wires of the basket before filling to the rim with further compost. The trailing Nasturtium looks decorative growing in this position, with scented Cottage Geraniums planted in the top. Watering has to be attended to regularly with hanging baskets, and they may need watering twice a day during very hot weather.

Terrace pots

Look out for fancy terracotta pots originally designed for the growing of strawberries or parsley in confined spaces. These pots are most suitable for the growing of the dwarf varieties of herbs and the natural colour of the containers given an antique charm to any courtyard or patio. If the pots are standing in a corner however, be sure that the pot is turned occasionally so that each little plant growing from the sockets of the pot receives a fair share of the sunlight.

When filling pots with plants, put in a layer of soil, then fit plants into one row of soil. Put in more soil and press down firmly, then put in another layer of plants, compost and so on until the pots are full and firmly planted. Water pots very frequently and carefully as they dry out quickly.

Stacking pots are also attractive and can be built up into tall towers or used in pairs or threesomes to give a variety of heights to a group of herbs.

Sage, Marigolds, Thyme and Parsley growing in terrace pots

PORCHES AND DOOR STEPS

A porch or at least a wide door step can be a useful site on which to place a small growing bag containing a selection of the more aromatic and colourful herbs, to welcome visitors.

If the doorstep is small, a home-made plant trough to fit each side of the door can look very attractive. Second-hand timber can often be bought quite cheaply at do-it-yourself shops and as long as a small sharp handsaw is available, the troughs can be constructed at home and made to fit the exact size of the doorstep. If the doorstep or porch is 1 m/40 in wide and measures 55 cm/22 in from back to front, six pieces of 12 mm/½ in timber ½ m/20 in long × 22 cm/9 in deep will make two troughs. Four end-pieces 15 cm/6 in × 30 cm/12 in or the actual depth of the troughs will complete the job. Nails a little longer than the thickness of the timber will be necessary. Make holes in the section of timber that will be the floor of the troughs, for drainage, and cover the holes with broken crock before filling the troughs with John Innes compost No 2 or 3. The troughs can stand on a brick at each corner, which will assist drainage. Dwarf herbs will look pretty growing in this situation, such as Golden Lemon Thyme, Dwarf White Lavender, or the prostrate Rosemary which grows only 15–30 cm/6–12 in high.

ABC of Herbs

Angelica

(Angelica archangelica)

Biennial which grows rather tall for containers, but is useful in the kitchen. The young green stems bear pale green leaves and tiny green-yellow flowers, which bloom in May and give an early touch of colour to a shady corner on a verandah or patio.

Cultivation

Seeds can be sown in August or March, but are best sown fresh from the plant rather than dried, when they become difficult to germinate. The plant likes a fairly damp situation, and will grow about 1.5 m/5 ft tall.

Uses

The roots and seeds of angelica are used commercially for distillation as they are rich in essential oils, and the flavouring is used in gin. Fresh leaf tips can be used to flavour jams, and particularly complement rhubarb, helping to remove tartness. Dried leaves are suitable for a tisane which has a settling effect on the digestive system and is a mildly stimulating tonic. The stems can be candied for cake decoration.

Anise

(Pimpinella anisum)

Annual which grows about 45 cm/18 in high and has white flowers in the summer.

Cultivation

Propagate by seed. Anise likes a fairly rich, well-drained soil and a sunny position. Do not transplant the seedlings once they are established. Results are sometimes disappointing, as the seed will only ripen in very warm summers. As soon as the plants have bloomed, the seeds will firm and ripen and the seed heads can then be collected and dried in the sun.

Uses

The leaves may be used to give an aniseed flavour to cooking, while the seeds have a penetrating flavour which should be used discreetly. Use aniseed to flavour puddings, bread, buns, soups, sauces, cream cheese and cabbage. Aniseed has the reputation of sweetening the breath and may be chewed.

BALM

(Melissa officinalis)

Perennial sometimes known as Sweet Balm, Lemon Balm or Melissa, which grows to a height of about 75 cm/2½ ft and is a good plant for windowbox or balcony with the lemon-like fragrance of its bright green crinkled leaves.

Cultivation

Only one plant is needed, as it spreads rapidly outwards, but can be divided to increase stock if necessary. This is a useful herb for growing in a position which receives sunlight for only a few hours daily in the summer, is reasonably moist

and has a little shelter. The seed may be sown in April or May, or a plant obtained instead. The plants die down in the winter months, but spring up early in the next year.

Uses

The flavour is softly spicy with a lemon scent, and leaves can be used in poulty and veal stuffings, and go well with mushrooms, delicate fish dishes and even mayonnaise. A few chopped leaves may be added to both vegetable and fruit salads. A soothing drink can be made from a few leaves infused in boiling water with a little lemon peel and honey, and is thought to relieve tiredness, induce relaxation, and counteract the onset of migraine.

BASIL

(Ocimum basilicum)

BUSH BASIL

(Ocimum minimum)

Annual in both forms. The larger plant, sometimes known as Sweet Basil, grows to 60 cm/2 ft high and has a small, whitish flowers. Bush Basil is much smaller, growing only 15 cm/6 in high.

Cultivation

Basil needs careful handling as the plants tend to damp off if the soil is too wet. It loves a sheltered, warm, sunny place. Sweet Basil should be grown from seed planted in the spring, and is best started in a greenhouse. The seedlings should be kept warm, well-fed and protected from draughts, and, once they get started, should be transferred to larger pots, as the plants are vigorous. Bush Basil is also rather tender, although ideal for sunny places and smaller containers.

Uses

Bush Basil has smaller leaves than Sweet Basil, but both have a deliciously scented clove flavour with a slightly peppery quality. Basil is excellent in all tomato dishes, pizza, omelettes and other egg dishes, spaghetti and rice, and with liver and sausages. Cooking releases a strong flavour, so Basil should be used with care or it may be overpowering.

Basil △   Basil

32

BAY

(Laurus nobilis)

Perennial sometimes known as Bay Laurel or Sweet Bay, and in favourable situations growing into a tree up to 12 m/40 ft high. A Bay tree is, however, suitable for growing in a large container as it can be clipped and shaped to a reasonable size.

Cultivation

New trees may be propagated by using half-ripe shoots as cuttings in late summer. These cuttings can be potted in small containers and make attractive little trees for tub growing for a few years more, before being planted in an open garden. Insert a cutting in a small pot containing peat and sand, watering as necessary. When the

plant has rooted, pot on into John Innes Potting Compost, using a 7 cm/3 in pot. The small tree can stay in this pot for up to a year before being potted again into a larger container. Bay trees do not like cold winds or hard frost, and may be moved indoors or into a greenhouse in winter.

Uses

The dark glossy leaves are thick, fleshy and aromatic. They may be used fresh or dried, and often half a leaf is enough to impart flavour. Bay is an essential ingredient of *bouquet garni*, and the leaves are used to flavour casseroles, soup, fish stock and milk puddings. A Bay leaf boiled with cauliflower helps to reduce cooking smells.

33

BERGAMOT

(Monarda didyma)

Perennial, sometimes known as Oswego, Bee Balm or Scarlet Monarda, grows to a height of about 60 cm/2 ft, and has decorative purple, lavender and crimson flowers. All parts of the plant are highly aromatic.

Cultivation

It is a good idea to obtain a plant from a nursery first, but plant stock can be increased by root division in the spring and autumn. Bergamot does best when protected from full sun, and

likes a warm, moist and fairly rich soil. During hot summer days, it should be watered regularly. Every part of the plant is aromatic and it is very attractive to bees.

Uses

The leaves can be used in small quantities in salads, and are sometimes added to pot pourri. Its best known use is to make Oswego or American Indian tea, from either the leaves or dried red flowers infused in boiling water for 5 minutes and sweetened with honey or sugar. This is considered to induce relaxation.

BORAGE

(Borago officinalis)

Annual which grows about 60 cm/2 ft high and is covered with black-eyed flowers of intense blue, sometimes shaded with pink. The leaves are rough and grey-green on thick strong stems, and have a cucumber flavour.

Cultivation

Borage grows easily from seed (and spreads rapidly by self-seeding), but the young seedlings like warmth, until the weather is suitable for putting them outside in light, well-drained soil with plenty of sun. Put the plants at the edge of containers as Borage throws spreading low growths from which the flowers hang in clusters and these will show off to added advantage over the edge of tubs. Although the plant is not highly aromatic, it attracts bees and is sometimes known as 'Beebread'. Continual cutting of the shoots will help to control its vigorous growth, and the trimmings can be used in the kitchen, or are attractive for flower arrangements.

Uses

Borage leaves and flowers are generally used fresh as they do not dry well. The leaves have a cucumber-flavour but are stringy in texture and not really suitable for salads. They give a subtle flavour to wine cups and fruit drinks when used as a garnish. The flowers may be candied by dipping in a sugar syrup.

BURNET

(Poterium sanguisorba)

Perennial, sometimes known as Salad Burnet, with large low-spreading leaves and copper-reddish flowers on stems reaching upwards to a height of 40 cm/15 in.

Cultivation

Seeds should be sown in April and the young seedlings transplanted when large enough to handle, or the plant may be increased by root-division. It is not fussy about soil, but does best on chalk, and is almost evergreen, with leaves lasting well into the winter and reappearing early in spring. The plant is attractive to bees, and the flowers are known as weather forecasters as they fold their petals and hide on a cloudy day before a storm.

Uses

Young fresh leaves may be chopped to sprinkle on salads, and have a light cucumber flavour. They may be used in omelettes, fish sauces and cream soups, and are used to garnish wine cups or cider drinks.

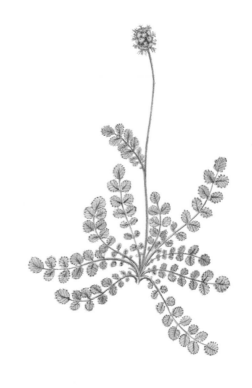

CAMOMILE

(Anthemis nobilis)

Perennial, sometimes known as Chamomile, or Roman Camomile, is often used for lawns in place of grass seed because of the pleasing fragrance when the lawn is walked upon.

Cultivation

The plant is attractive to set in tiny crevices on a terrace, or can be used to make paths. If there are cracks in or between paving stones, scrape out as much soil and stone as possible and insert rich potting compost. Plant the little seedlings in June or July in damp weather, and if possible make sure that the crown of the plant remains on the surface of the compost. Firm planting is essential and plants should be watered often until they are growing well. Plants can be raised from seed sown in April, and a small lawn can be made from plants placed about 10 cm/4 ins apart.

Uses

Camomile is a traditional healing herb, but the best oil for this purpose is extracted from the annual variety, Matricaria recutita. Camomile leaves or flowers may be sprinkled in the bath for reviving effects, and shampoos made with Camomile flowers are particularly recommended for blonde hair. Camomile has a bitter flavour, but the flowers are used for a soothing digestive drink. Use about 5 fresh flower heads or 3 dried heads infused in half a cupful of boiling water.

Caraway

(Carum carvi)

Biennial producing flowers and seed heads in the second year, following spring sowing.

Cultivation

Sow seeds in May in a sunny, well-drained place and thin out seedlings to about 27 cm/9 in apart. Water well in dry weather and expect an attractive display of feathery leaves, reaching a height of about 40 cm/15 in. The flower heads will ripen in succession and the stems supporting them can be cut at soil level before being hung up to

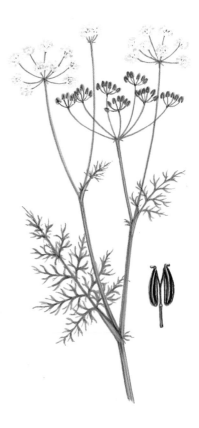

dry. Enclose the seedhead in a small paper bag before hanging, to collect any dry seeds as they fall.

Uses

Caraway seeds have a strong aromatic flavour which people either love or hate. They are used to flavour a number of liqueurs, notably Kummel, and are used for cakes, sweets and biscuits, and for flavouring bread. Caraway seeds are also used in soups and stews, and to flavour turnips, cabbage and baked apples. They are good blended with cream cheese or blue cheese.

CHERVIL

(Anthriscus cerefolium)

Annual which is quick-growing and hardy, with feathery and aniseed-flavoured leaves and attractive white flowers. The plant grows about 45 cm/18 in high.

Cultivation

Seeds can be sown at four-weekly intervals to give a succession of green leaves, and they may be sown right through the winter months behind glass, in a warm kitchen to provide leaves for flavouring during the winter. This is one of

the earliest herbs to appear and is traditionally associated with Eastertide dishes. Chervil likes the shade, so is useful for growing on balconies or in windowboxes which receive very little sunshine.

Uses

Chervil can be used as a garnish, or chopped in salads, egg mayonnaise, omelettes, soup, chicken and fish dishes. It sets off the flavour of other herbs and so is useful in mixtures of herbs to sprinkle on vegetables or use in sauces.

CHIVES

(Allium schoenoprasum)

Perennial of the onion family, with a light onion flavour. They look like clumps of grass and will grow in any type of container or in a pot on a windowsill or with other herbs in a larger plant trough.

Cultivation

Chives are easily grown from seed sown in April or by division of plants, and they will do best in a medium light soil with some moisture and a little shade. The plants form a cluster of small

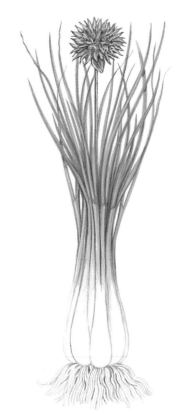

bulbs at the root, and the main clumps can be divided to give pieces of three or four shoots to make new plants every two or three years.

Uses

The leaves may be snipped with scissors for flavouring right through the summer. When the flowers begin to appear, they should be cut off as they retard growth when the leaves are needed for cooking, but it is worth keeping one plant in flower as the flowers dry well for winter flower arrangements.

Chop Chive leaves to sprinkle on cream soups, to make savoury butter for use with meat, poultry or fish, and to sprinkle on salads or seafood cocktails, or blend into cream cheese.

COMFREY

(Symphytum officinale)

Perennial, which is long-living and has a high quantity of vegetable protein. It will grow to about 75 cm/2½ ft if allowed to, but if the large ovate leaves are often picked, the height of the plant will be kept under control.

Cultivation

Seed may be sown at any time of the year and the seedlings will transplant readily. If a few leaves are left soaking in a bucket of water for a couple of weeks to ferment, the liquid is an excellent fertiliser for other plants and can be used for other herbs growing in containers.

Uses

Comfrey was reputedly used to heal broken bones, sprains and bruises, and is considered useful to treat lung complaints, whooping cough and internal haemorrhage. The leaves of Comfrey can be cooked as a replacement for cabbage.

CORIANDER

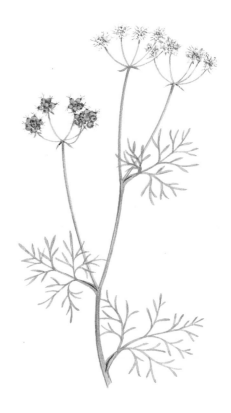

(Coriandum sativum)

Annual similar to Caraway, which grows to a height of 45 cm/18 in and is a slender but sparsely-branched hardy plant with tiny, very pale purple flowers appearing in July and August.

Cultivation

The seeds are sown in April and will yield ripe seed for harvesting in August. Leaves, flowers and unripe seeds give off a strong smell which many people do not care for, but the seeds are pleasantly aromatic when ripe. As the seeds are

produced in the first year, quick production warrants the herbs being grown in a large container. The plants prefer light, warm soil and sunshine.

Uses

The aromatic seeds have a fresh flavour of orange and the flavour increases when the whole seedheads are dried. The seeds may be used whole or crushed into powder and the delicate flavour is often used in curry. The flavouring may be used in soups and in dishes made with pork, duck, goose, game and beef. It may also be used in pickling spices, and for giving a subtle flavour to cakes, biscuits, custards and mousses. The leaves may be used in Indian cookery and salads.

Cottage Geranium

(Pelargonium)

Perennial, available in about a dozen different varieties, each with highly scented, delicately shaped leaves, but insignificant flowers. They are very beautiful and fragrant, especially those of the Rose, Lemon and Peppermint varieties, and grow well in all types of containers.

Cultivation

Buy plants of one or two types and take cuttings to increase stock. A flower pot containing John Innes Potting Compost and a little sand will help the cuttings to root, which they will do in about six weeks if taken from the parent plant during March to May.

Uses

As the leaves dry and fall off, collect them to use in pot pourri. The leaves are highly aromatic, and one or two will give a delicate flavour to apple jelly. A fresh leaf put in a cake tin before sponge mixture is poured in and baked, will make the sponge cake most delicious, and a leaf can also be used to scent junkets, creams and mousses.

Dandelion

(Taraxacum officinale)

Perennial

Cultivation

Dandelion can be grown from seed sown in April, and then thinned to 30 cm/1 ft apart. Seed heads should be cut from the plants after flowering so that self-sown plants are eliminated. Dandelions succeed in almost any soil, provided it is not too moist.

Uses

For salads, the leaves should be blanched, which can be easily done in the open air if they are covered, as soon as growth appears, with a thick blanket of straw, or with an upturned flowerpot (put a stone over the hole in each pot to exclude all light). The plants should be watered, but not made over-wet, and the leaves will be ready in about two weeks.

The leaves make a delicious salad, rather like Chicory in flavour. Mature leaves may be infused in boiling water, using 500 ml/1 pt of water to 25 g/1 oz of leaves, to make Dandelion tea. Roots which are gathered in the autumn may be washed, but not peeled, and then baked in the oven to a deep brown colour. When they are cold, they may be ground and used as coffee.

DILL

(Anethum graveolens)

Annual which is hardy, and has an appearance similar to fennel. The plant grows about 45 cm/ 18 in high and has feathery blue-green leaves and yellow flowers.

Cultivation

Dill grows from seeds sown in April and May and can be thinned to 27 cm/10 in apart in a medium soil which is neither too dry nor wet and has a fair amount of sunshine. Keep the plant well away from Fennel when both are in the early stages as they look very similar and may cross-fertilise.

Uses

Dill is widely used in herbal medicines to stimulate the system, settle the digestion and soothe the stomach, and is used to relieve flatulence in children. It has a penetrating aromatic scent which seems to be a combination of anise and caraway but is lighter and more lemony.

The leaves and seeds may both be used for flavouring and are important in Scandinavian recipes. Finely chopped leaves are good in white sauce to go with chicken, lamb or eggs, or can be used in omelettes and salads, or sprinkled on hot new potatoes. and on potato salad. Dill is particularly delicious with fish (especially oily fish such as mackerel), salmon and shellfish. A sprig of Dill or some Dill seeds may be included in cucumber or cauliflower pickles, and the leaves may be infused in wine vinegar to make a lightly flavoured vinegar for dressings. Chewed dill seeds help to sweeten the breath.

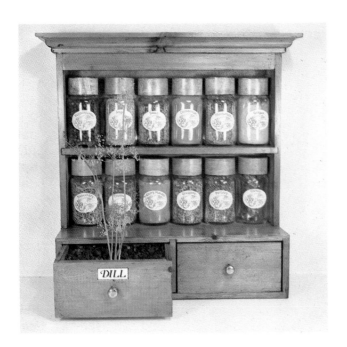

FENNEL

(Foeniculum vulgare)

Perennial and closely related to Dill.

Cultivation

Seeds should be sown in April in soil which is not too damp, nor clay-like, and which will get plenty of warmth. Plants can be kept down to about 30 cm/1 ft in height, but will grow to about 15 m/5 ft, and are very decorative. A bronze variety is available which is particularly attractive as a contrast to other herb plants, and useful for flower decoration. The plant has thick polished stems and feathery foliage.

Florence Fennel or Finocchio is of the same family but is an annual, the root of which is used as a vegetable.

Uses

The feathery leaves are mainly used in the kitchen, and have a flavour which is a combination of anise and celery, particularly associated with fish cookery. Fennel is good with oily fish as it has digestive properties, and it may be used in fish stuffings, or grilled or baked with the fish. It may also be used in a white sauce with fish, or can be added to gooseberry sauce to serve with mackerel. Fennel seeds are good sprinkled on cheese savouries, and on sauerkraut.

GARLIC

(Allium sativum)

Annual of the onion family, which grows in clusters like shallots from the planting of single 'cloves' or segments into which the large clustered bulb can be broken.

Cultivation

Garlic can be planted in a container, such as a plastic bucket, if drainage holes are made in the bottom, and this can hold three or four plants which will be ready for harvesting in late July or August. Plant the cloves 2.5 cm/1 in deep in good quality compost or light soil in March, and put in a place where there is plenty of sun but some moisture. One clove could be planted in a flowerpot for the kitchen windowsill, if there is little space outside. When the cloves have formed clusters, the plants should be pulled up and hung in bunches in a covered, dry place until they are really dry and the bulbs are solid.

Uses

Garlic was reputed to keep vampires at a distance and many people find it repellant. A little Garlic used with subtlety can, however, add zest and flavour to savoury cooking. The cloves should be peeled and then either crushed in a special squeezer or with a kitchen knife. A clove of Garlic may be rubbed round the inside of a salad bowl to give a subtle hint of flavour to the salad. Crushed Garlic fried in oil or butter adds zest to soups, sauces and gravy, and Garlic is essential to the cooking of Southern France and

Italy. Those who enjoy Garlic say that a regular intake helps to keep the chest clear and fends off colds, and it has strong antiseptic and germicidal qualities, often having been used to speed the healing of wounds.

HYSSOP

(Hyssopus officinalis)

Perennial small shrub which is hardy, bearing dark green leaves on thick woody stems, with pink, blue or white flowers and a scent which attracts bees. Generally the plant grows about 50 cm/2 ft high, but a dwarf variety called Hyssopus aristatus is most suited for growing in small pockets in stone walling on a verandah or patio.

Cultivation

Propagation can be by seed sown in April or May and by green cuttings taken in summer. The plant prefers a light soil and sunny position. The shrub can be trimmed severely in autumn and spring without affecting growth.

Uses

Hyssop is associated with cleansing and purification and was one of the herbs strewn on floors and used in nosegays carried for protection against infectious diseases. The herb is not much used in the kitchen, although it can be finely chopped to give a minty flavour to salads, game and meat, and is one of the ingredients of *Chartreuse* liqueur.

LAVENDER

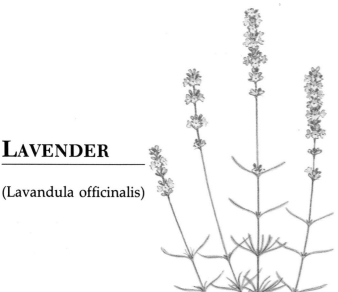

(Lavandula officinalis)

Perennial of which there are many varieties. For small areas and containers, the dwarf varieties are particularly useful. Dwarf White (Lavandula nana alba) is a charming miniature shrub growing 15–20 cm/6–8 in high and is a beautiful choice for a sink garden or verandah, with tiny white flowers. Lavandula atropurpurea nana has silver-grey foliage and purple-violet flowers, and is a good choice for edgings or larger herb containers. Dwarf Munstead is another choice to consider although this one will grow 45 cm/18 in high, making a good border shrub for path edgings.

Cultivation

Two or three well-established plants from a nursery of different types of Lavender can be bought, and then cuttings taken from each plant to increase stock. After flowering, roots and shoots will appear from the bottom of the parent plant. These should be carefully pulled off when about 10 cm/4 in long and one or two bottom leaves taken off. These little plants can then be put around the edge of a 15 cm/6 in flowerpot and a plastic cover placed over the top, to save them from harsh weather conditions. If the cuttings are taken in September, they should develop into plenty of new Lavender plants for transplanting the following March. If they do not look very strong, leave them until the following September before moving.

Lavender is not completely hardy, but it will grow for many years if young growth is clipped back to reshape the bush once the flowers have been picked in August. Old wood should not be cut as Lavender does not like mutilation, but a compact shrub will better resist frost damage during the winter.

Uses

Lavender is not used much in the kitchen, although the flowers can be candied, but is an essential ingredient of pot pourri.

Lemon Verbena

(Aloysia citriodora)

Perennial lemon-scented deciduous shrub, which is ideal for tub-growing, if the container can be given some protection against a harsh winter, by covering both the tub and the soil inside, as well as the shoots of the plant. This very tender aromatic shrub will appreciate this attention and, although it may look very dead through the winter months, small knobs of green buds will appear and make fresh growths in the spring. The light yellow-green leaves have a strong scent, and there are spikes of mixed white and mauve flowers.

Cultivation

New plants can be obtained from seed sown in the spring and and transplanted in the summer, or new young shoots may be used as cuttings. The plant does best in a rather poor soil, in a sheltered position and grows 90 cm/3 ft or more high. The plant can be moved indoors in the winter, and kept in a warm room.

Uses

Lemon Verbena leaves may be made into a refreshing tea served either hot or cold, with a sedative effect on the nose and throat. The leaves will also give a lemon flavour to fruit drinks, jellies, sauces for fish, poultry or white meat, or may be placed at the bottom of a cake tin before the sponge mixture is poured in and baked. The leaves can also be used to scent linen and to make pot pourri.

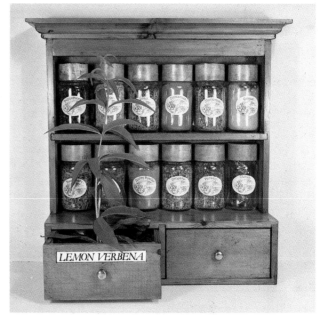

MARJORAM

(Origanum majorana and Origanum onites)

Perennial (Origanum onites or Pot Marjoram) is hardy, growing to about 60 cm/2 ft high, and will spread and layer itself. Origanum majorana or Sweet Marjoram (sometimes known as Knotted Marjoram) is also a perennial, but needs to be treated as a half-hardy annual in Britain because it seldom survives a wet cold winter. It will grow about 30 cm/1 ft high.

Cultivation

Pot Marjoram can be grown from seed or cuttings taken in the early spring and likes a warm,

light, well-drained soil in a warm sheltered position. Sweet Marjoram will grow from seeds sown in the spring, but is often slow to germinate. Both plants have aromatic leaves and pretty pink, white or mauve flowers, and are closely related to Oregano, which is wild Marjoram commonly specified for Italian and Greek recipes.

Uses

Sweet Marjoram has the mildest and most pleasant flavour, with a spicy, warm flavour similar to cloves. It may be used in herb mixtures, added to tomato and mushroom dishes, pizza, lamb, pork, veal and chicken. Marjoram is also good in vegetable soups, and with courgettes, aubergines and potatoes.

51

MINT

(Mentha)

Perennial with many different varieties including: Ginger Mint, Horse Mint, White Peppermint, Black Peppermint, Curly Mint, Eau de Cologne Mint, Pennyroyal, Spearmint, Round-leaved Mint, Pineapple Mint and Bowles Mint. Mint has a habit of spreading its roots far and wide, making life difficult for any other herb which may be growing with it in any piece of earth or container.

Spearmint

Peppermint

Cultivation

It is advisable to buy a root of Mint in a nursery rather than bother with seed, and it is pleasant to select two or three different kinds, so that there is always variety for the kitchen or other purposes. If it is intended that the Mint should be grown in a window box or a tub with other herbs, it is a good idea to repot the roots into a slightly larger pot than the original one, and this larger pot should then be planted in the windowbox or tub. This means that the Mint roots will be entirely contained in the flowerpot and will not spread and dominate other plants. Every other spring, dig up the pot from the large container and remove the potbound Mint. Break off small pieces of the plant and repot then in fresh soil before plunging them back into the larger container. Spearmint roots can be repotted and brought indoors for the winter, and will give a small supply of fresh leaves throughout the winter months. Many of the different Mints can be grown together for attractive effects. Try Ginger Mint and Round-Leaved Mint. The very fragrant ones such as Eau de Cologne and Pineapple Mints are particularly worth growing for their highly-scented leaves which can be dried for pot pourri.

Uses

Spearmint is most commonly used in the kitchen for Mint sauce to accompany lamb, and for Mint jelly. A few Mint leaves make a pretty garnish for fruit salads, fruit cocktails, grapefruit halves, alcoholic fruit cups and soups. The leaves may be crystallised to use as a garnish for cakes and sweets.

NASTURTIUM

(Tropaeolum majus)

Annual which is easy and colourful to grow in window boxes and other containers. It has a trailing habit, so looks very attractive, with its bright yellow, orange and dark red flowers, cascading from a plant trough or growing on a windowsill.

Cultivation

Sow the seeds in spring where there is plenty of sun but rather poor soil. The plants tend to self-sow and spread. There is also a Dwarf Nasturtium (Tropaeolum minus) which is suitable for container growing. These can be planted in small growing bags on a windowsill, but if the growing compost is very rich, there will be more leaves than flowers.

Uses

Nasturtium leaves and flowers can be used fresh for salads and sandwiches, and for sprinkling on potatoes. They are rather peppery and the leaves should be chopped finely. Try mixing them with cream cheese, but do not leave the mixture too long or it will become bitter. Young green Nasturtium seeds can be pickled as a substitute for capers.

PARSLEY

(Petroselinum crispium)

Biennial whcih will grow easily in a windowbox or tub, or a special pot with small pockets of soil, or round the edges of containers.

Cultivation

It is recommended that the seed should be sown very thinly where the plants are to mature, but for containers it may be necessary to sow the seed and then transplant the parsley when the plants are large enough. They should be kept moist and well watered for a few days after planting. Have a good rich potting compost in which to sow parsley seed; sow thinly, and cover the seed lightly, keeping the soil moist. Parsley has a long germination period and may take eight weeks to start growing. It is said that, 'Parsley grows for the wicked but not for the just . The seed is best sown in May, and although the plant is biennial, it is worth making a new sowing each year. The plant lasts well into the winter if it is not allowed to flower and kept well-picked to prevent coarse growth forming.

Uses

Parsley is a good source of Vitamin C and iron, and is reputed to be a tonic, a digestive stimulant, and a help to those suffering from rheumatism. Crisp Parsley is an attractive garnish for cooked dishes, and blends well with other herbs in mixtures – it is one of the herbs essential for *bouquet garni*.

PENNYROYAL

(Mentha pulegium)

Perennial member of the Mint family which grows only 15 cm/6 in high and likes a shady situation. It can be planted between paving stones like Camomile, and is useful for a sink garden, forming a creeping mat of small light-green leaves. It can be planted as a small lawn, which will give off a peppermint smell when walked upon, and only needs cutting twice a year.

Cultivation

The plant can be propagated by root division, and small tufts of the plant should be placed 15 cm/6 in apart in spring or autumn. During the summer, Pennyroyal has erect branched flowering stems, about a foot high, of mauve flowers.

Uses

The flavour of pennyroyal is strong, but it can be used occasionally to flavour stuffings and soups, or to sprinkle on buttered new potatoes.

PURSLANE

(Portulaca oleracea)

Annual which likes a really hot dry soil, and is ideal for a windowbox which has the sun for most of the day in the summer.

Cultivation

Sow the seed in a small pot about late March and cover with a small piece of glass, or stand the pot inside a polythene bag. Water the seeds well until the seedlings show through the soil, and also after transplanting to larger containers. The addition of a handful of sharp sand to the growing compost is much appreciated by this plant. Sowings may be made monthly to ensure a continuous crop of the thick fleshy leaves. If the plants are cut frequently, they continue to produce fresh leaves, but should not be allowed to flower. There is a slightly less hardy golden-leaved variety which is decorative in containers.

Uses

Purslane leaves should be stripped from their stalks to use in salads, or to be made into soup with some sorrel. The leaves make good sandwiches with brown bread and butter, and the stalks used to be cooked and pickled in sweetened vinegar.

POT MARIGOLD

(Calendula officinalis)

Annual with the brightest flowers of all the culinary herbs, and very decorative for growing in pots and tubs, or in small borders.

Cultivation

Seeds should be sown in March or April and do best in loamy soil with plenty of sun. The plants should be thinned out to about 30 cm/1 ft apart and will reach a height of about 30 cm/1 ft. They tend to self-sow if allowed to, and it is worth leaving them to seed if there is space.

Uses

The leaves used to be used in the kitchen, but they are very strong with an acrid aftertaste. The petals give a rich pleasant flavour to soups, stews and gravy, can be sprinkled on salads or mixed with cream cheese. They are colourful used to garnish potatoes and rice, and are sometimes used to colour cakes. The petals can be dried for winter use to garnish lentil and barley soups.

ROSEMARY

(Rosemarinus Officinalis)

Perennial evergreen shrub, quite capable of living twenty years or more, with narrow, dark, grey-green leaves, blue flowers, and a beautiful resinous fragrance. After flowering in April and May, the shrub can be clipped to keep the height required for tub-growing. The clippings can be dried so that the leaves can be used for culinary or fragrant purposes.

Cultivation

Cuttings may be taken in March or September, and growth will be slow at first, which can be an advantage if space is limited. Rosemary enjoys a dry sunny position, with a little shelter, and a light, fairly sandy or chalky soil.

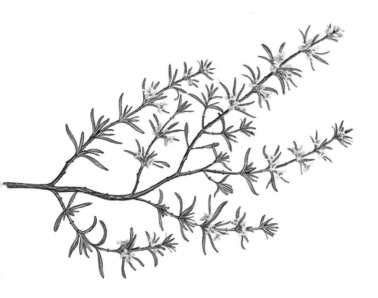

Uses

This is the herb of friendship and remembrance and was often carried by bridesmaids at weddings, included in the decorations and dipped in the festive wine. Rosemary is widely used in hair shampoos, tonics and oils as it is thought to stimulate hair growth and improve its condition. Sprigs of Rosemary may be burned to purify the air, and are delightful in pot pourri.

The plant has a strong scent and flavour, and a sprig laid on a joint of lamb, pork or veal while roasting makes the meat delicious. It is also good used sparingly with duck or pheasant, and to flavour stuffings, omelettes and soups, or to garnish alcoholic fruit or cider cups. Many Greek recipes incorporate Rosemary.

SAGE

(Salvia officinalis)

Perennial bushy wide-spreading plant with grey-green leaves and pretty blue or pinkish flowers. There are a number of varieties, and the golden-leaved and red-leaved are particularly decorative. It will grow in any type of container including flower pots, and looks most attractive growing in a windowbox.

Cultivation

Seeds may be sown in the early summer, and when the seedlings are growing strongly they should be pricked out into separate little pots (ice cream or yogurt containers may be used), and then moved to a more permanent position later in the year. Sage likes the sun, but is not fussy about soil conditions. The shrub will produce a large number of side shoots and tender branches can be pulled off and used for flavour-ing, or dried for winter use. If regular use is made of the shoots, the shrub will not grow straggly and need only be renewed every three or four years by taking cuttings or by root division.

Uses

Sage has a strong aromatic fragrance and flavour and is said to ensure long life. It is a powerful herb to use in cooking, and is excellent for helping the digestion of rich fatty foods. Sage and onion stuffing is the traditional accompaniment to duck and goose, and sage also goes well with pork and ham mixtures, with sausages, pies and liver. It is good with cheese, and is an ingredient of Sage Derby cheese.

Savory

(Satureia hortensis and Satureia montana)

Annual Satureia hortensis (Summer Savory) is dainty but delicate, with lilac-coloured flowers borne above medium-sized leaves. It grows to about 27 cm/9 in high and is a plant which can be grown around the edge of a windowbox or larger plant container on a balcony, giving a very pleasing effect. Winter Savory is a perennial which makes a bush plant about 45 cm/18 in high. Both plants are attractive to bees.

Summer Savory

Summer Savory

Cultivation

Summer Savory should be sown in the spring and transplanted as soon as frosts are not likely, and the plants should flower in July. It will grow in the winter in a warm room if the container is kept near a window so that the plant has the advantage of winter sunshine. Winter Savory can be grown from division of plants in spring or autumn, and likes poor, light well-drained soil in full sun.

Use

Summer Savory is known as the 'bean herb', as it goes well with all kinds of beans, but particularly broad beans. Both kinds are rather similar to Thyme or Marjoram in flavour and are useful in any mixture of herbs for stuffing pork, veal or poultry. Savory is also good in strongly flavoured game soups, stews and cooked cheese dishes.

SORREL

(Rumex scutatus)

Perennial sometimes known as French Sorrel. There is also Garden Sorrel and Wood Sorrel, but the French variety is most suitable for kitchen use.

Cultivation

The seeds or divided plants may be put in place in the spring, and the plant only takes 60 days

French Sorrel

Wood Sorrel

from sowing to maturity, while a plant will last for at least five years producing a good quantity of leaves. Sorrel is low-growing if the French variety is chosen, being about 15 cm/6 in high, which is excellent for container growing. If blossom is required, the Garden Sorrel has a pinkish flower.

Uses

Sorrel has crisp green leaves with a slightly lemon flavour which is delicate, but with a bitter undertone and as acidity which is very refreshing. It can be cooked like spinach as a vegetable, used in spinach, pea or chicken soups, or as soup on its own.

Tarragon

(Artemisia dracunculus)

Perennial which can be destroyed by a hard frost. On a balcony or patio, there is usually enough shelter to keep the containers protected, and the plants can be covered with a little straw during the winter months.

Cultivation

Tarragon can only be grown from roots, as the flowers are sterile, so it will be necessary to buy the first plant for cuttings. Try to take a *heel* attached to the cuttings and, after pressing them firmly into the compost around the edge of a

small flowerpot, put the pot in a shady spot. The cuttings will then make strong roots. They should be taken in June and will be ready for transplanting the following spring. Tarragon will look and produce best in a fairly large container as it grows to a height of about 60 cm/2 ft. French Tarragon is spicier and better-flavoured, but tends to lose flavour if left in the same place for more than a couple of years. Russian Tarragon is hardier and grows larger, but the flavour is not so good.

Uses

Tarragon does not dry very well and is best used fresh, particularly in classic French recipes. It is particularly valuable in sauces, and for making Tarragon butter to go with meat, poultry or fish. A simple roast chicken is delicious if cooked with nothing but a few sprays of Tarragon and some butter. Tarragon vinegar is useful for making salad dressing.

THYME

(Thymus vulgaris and many others)

Perennial neat little evergreen shrub with wiry stems, which can be obtained in many varieties. Thymus vulgaris (Common thyme) is most widely used, and grows into a neat bush about 30 cm/1 ft high with tiny lilac flowers. Lemon thyme (Thymus citriodorus) and Golden Lemon thyme (Thymus citriodorus aureus) are both delightful, with their light leaves and strong lemon scent.

Cultivation

Seeds may be sown in April, or slips pulled from established plants in the summer, but the slips must have some roots and be planted firmly. It likes warmth and a chalky, dry, well-drained soil in sunshine, and will grow well in cracks in pathways or in crevices in walls.

Uses

Thyme is one of the ingredients of *bouquet garni* and mixes with parsley for poultry and veal stuffings. The delicate flavour goes well with vegetables, and it helps in the digestion of rich fatty meats and poultry. Lemon Thyme is particularly good with fish and chicken, and may also be used to flavour custards and creams. If grown near a beehive, it is supposed to give a delicious flavour to honey.

Yarrow

(Achillea millefolium)

Perennial growing about 45 cm/18 in high which is an ideal subject for growing in confined places. The plant has fine-cut foliage and white, scented flowers in July.

Cultivation

Grow from seeds sown in May. The seedlings should be transplanted when large enough.

Uses

Yarrow tea made from the leaves is excellent for severe colds, and the plant is highly decorative for flower arrangements.

Bay, Rosemary and Thyme prepared for drying

HARVESTING, DRYING, FREEZING AND STORING

HARVESTING

For everyday use, herbs may be picked when needed. A light trimming of straggly plants will give enough leaves for kitchen use during the growing season, and will also help to keep the plants tidy. The main harvest of herbs for storage is made during the summer and autumn, according to whether leaves or seeds are wanted. During the growing season, cut sprigs 6–8 in long from the end of the stems; this will encourage side shoots and give bushy growth for the later harvest.

The first harvesting should be just before the herbs come into flower, but harvesting can continue later if growth is vigorous. Herbs can be cut back to about one-third of their growth at each cutting and then should be allowed to recover before the next cutting. Leaves should be cut on stems when the sun has dried off dew or rain, but before the full heat of the sun starts to extract too much herbal fragrance. Tarragon should be cut when young and about 30 cm/1 ft high, otherwise the leaves may be bitter. Sage may be cut for a long period from early spring to late autumn. Rosemary is best cut in late summer when the spires have fully developed, while bay can be cut all the year round (but mature leaves dry best). Borage, Camomile flowers and Marigold petals are dried. Dill, Anise, Caraway and Coriander are left until the seed heads ripen, although the leaves may be used for flavouring during the summer. Garlic bulbs are lifted when the leaves are dead.

DRYING

Leaves

Pick stems of herbs when the leaves are to be dried. Tie small bunches of each herb with thin string or cotton and put a small piece of paper over the top to prevent dust falling on the leaves. Hang in a warm, dry, dark place which is well ventilated and with good circulation of air to carry away evaporating moisture. Do not expose herbs to extremes of heat or they may turn brown and lose flavour. If a drying place is too light, it will affect the volatile oil content and lessen scent and flavour. Thick fleshy leaves will take longer to dry than small thin ones.

If there is space, the herbs can be spread out on a piece of muslin or cheesecloth stretched on a rack and placed in an airing cupboard which maintains an even heat between 27°–37°C/80°–100°F. All leaves should be dried on their stems, except bay leaves which should be taken off stems and spread out for drying. The herbs are ready for storage when they are crisp enough to rub off their stems, but they should still be green and fresh-smelling, and taste like fresh herbs when liquid is added.

Each herb should be dried separately, but may be mixed for storage. If a number of herbs are being dried at the same time, label each rack or bunch carefully as they can be difficult to identify when dried. Rub the leaves from the stems with the fingers or by rolling lightly with a rolling pin, and store in small dark glass jars in a cool dry place. Try to use dried herbs within a year as flavour deteriorates gradually.

Parsley is difficult to dry and needs special treatment. It should be picked so that there are two or three groups of leaves on each stem. Put the Parsley into a bowl and pour on boiling water. Take out at once and pat dry quickly with a clean tea towel. Heat the oven to 200°C/400°F/ Gas Mark 6 and take out the oven racks. Hang the little bunches of Parsley leaves over the racks, spreading them out well. Put into the oven for just one minute. Remove from racks and put on to a muslin covered rack, as other herbs, to finish off the drying in a warm cupboard. This will give crisp, bright green Parsley.

Flowers

Flowers should be quite dry when picked and fully open, but not wilted or discoloured. It may be necessary to pick just a few at a time rather than waiting for them all to be ready at the same time. Handle them gently and do not wash them. Spread out carefully to dry. Use the same muslin-covered racks to dry flowers and Marigold petals, but make sure air circulates as flowers and petals are very fleshy and give off a lot of moisture. Rose petals may be dried this way too for making pot pourri. Petals should be dried until they are crisp, without any stickiness. Lavender should be cut with long stems when in full bloom and will dry very well standing in jars, so that it can be used to decorate and scent a room while drying. For use in Lavender bags or pot pourri, the flowers can be rubbed from the stems when the stems are completely dry and brittle.

Seeds

The seeds of Anise, Caraway, Coriander, Dill and Fennel are ready to harvest when the seed capsules turn brown, and they should be cut on a warm dry day. Cut off the whole seedhead about half way down the stem. Tie the stems in a bunch and cover the seedheads with a paper bag, allowing plenty of air inside. Hang in a cool dry place until all the seeds have fallen into the bag. Spread the seeds on trays and leave in an airy room covered with thick paper for 2 weeks before putting into jars. They should be hard and difficult to break with a finger nail, and must not smell musty or they are not completely dry.

FREEZING

While drying is particularly suitable for the twiggy shrubs such as Thyme, Sage and Rosemary, the tender-leaved herbs like Mint, Basil and Chives freeze such better. Parsley, Fennel and Dill are also suitable for freezing, or mixtures such as *bouquet garni* and *fines herbes* can be prepared ready for speedy cooking.

There are two good ways of freezing herbs. For the first method, cut sprigs of young leaves, wash and shake off surplus moisture. Put on a tray in the freezer for a few minutes so that they harden and then pack in small bags of each variety for storage. Put the small bags into a larger bag for easy handling in the freezer. These herbs may be crumbled into dishes without thawing, but will not be useful for garnishing as their crispness is lost. Small bunches of Parsley, Thyme and Bayleaf can be tied together with cotton and packed in the freezer to use as *bouquet garni*.

A better way of freezing herbs is to chop them finely and pack into ice-cube trays with a little water to cover. Freeze and then wrap each cube in a twist of foil before packing into polythene bags for freezer storage. The whole cube may be put into soups or stews, or a cube can be thawed in a sieve so that excess moisture drains away before the chopped herbs are used. This method is particularly useful for Mint and Parsley which are often needed in large quantities for sauces.

ge, Thyme, Chives and dried Lavender make an attractive display on kitchen shelves

HERBS IN THE KITCHEN

A small selection of fresh and dried herbs will help to improve the most simple recipes right through the year. A few sprigs of fresh leaves can be picked at any time, and the bulk of the herbs may be dried in the summer. Dried herbs are about three times as strong as fresh ones, but the fresh ones will release more flavour if lightly crushed or chopped before being added to dishes. Dried herbs should also be crushed and soaked in a little liquid from the recipe before being added to the dish.

Herbs used to be chosen for flavouring according to where they grew e.g. lamb from the lowlands was flavoured with wild Mint which grew near the pastures, while mountain lamb was paired with wild Thyme or Marjoram. Many foods are traditionally paired with certain herbs, such as sage with fatty meat and poultry as it helps digestion, but the choice is highly individual and there are usually a number of possible variations. Herb flavouring should never be so strong that it overpowers a dish, but it should serve to bring out the flavour of the main ingredients. Some mixtures of herbs are useful for general flavouring purposes.

FLAVOURINGS

Bouquet garni is usually made up of a sprig of Thyme, a sprig of Parsley and a Bayleaf, with sometimes a sprig of Marjoram. These little bouquets can be tied with cotton and stored for use in soups and stews. A mixture of the appropriate herbs may be rubbed finely and made up in tiny muslin or cheesecloth bags. These are very convenient to store in jars.

Fines herbes is a mixture often needed for salads and for egg dishes such as omelettes. The mixture includes finely chopped Parsley, Chervil, Chives and Tarragon.

Mixed herbs consist of a mixture of more coarsely flavoured herbs which is used for many recipes. The mixture should be Sage, Parsley, Marjoram, and Thyme. To select the most appropriate herbs to complement favourite foods, follow this checklist.
Beef – Rosemary, Savory, Marjoram, Thyme
Lamb – Mint, Rosemary, Marjoram, Dill, Savory
Pork – Sage, Rosemary, Marjoram
Veal – Rosemary, Sage, Savory, Lemon Thyme, Lemon Balm
Ham – Parsley, Marjoram, Sage
Chicken – Parsley, Tarragon, Thyme, Marjoram

Duck and Goose – Sage, Thyme, Rosemary, Savory

Fish – Basil, Chervil, Chives, Thyme, Fennel, Mint, Sage, Dill, Parsley

Cheese – Basil, Caraway, Chives, Dill, Marjoram, Mint, Tarragon, Thyme, Sage

Eggs – Basil, Chervil, Chives, Marjoram, Parsley, Tarragon, Thyme

Beans – Savory

Cucumber – Mint, Parsley, Chives, Dill

Tomatoes – Basil, Mint, Parsley, Chives

Onions – Sage

Salads – Basil, Borage, Chervil, Chives, Dill, Fennel, Lemon Balm, Mint, Parsley, Savory, Tarragon

Vegetables – Basil, Chives, Fennel, Mint, Parsley, Rosemary, Savory, Tarragon

Fruit – Borage, Lemon Balm, Mint, Rosemary

HERB SEASONINGS

If plenty of herbs can be harvested and dried, it is convenient to make up some bottles of mixed herb seasoning which can be kept near the cooker. A pinch or two of the powdered seasoning will enliven many savoury dishes and save time searching for individual jars and packets.

To make **pungent seasoning** use 50 g/2 oz dried orange peel to 25 g/1 oz each of dried Marjoram, Thyme and Hyssop. The peel can be made by taking strips of orange skin without the white pith and drying them at the bottom of a cool oven until crisp. The peel and the herbs can be rubbed to a coarse powder with a rolling pin or an electric blender.

To make **sweet herb seasoning**, use 50 g/2 oz each of dried Parsley, Marjoram and Chervil mixed with 25 g/1 oz each of dried Thyme, Lemon Thyme, Basil and Savory, and 12 g/½ oz dried Tarragon. The herbs should be rubbed to a coarse powder and put into an airtight jar.

HERB VINEGARS

Herb-flavoured vinegar is useful in the kitchen to give a special flavour to salad dressings and mayonnaise. Tarragon, Fennel, Mint, Marjoram, Basil and Dill are excellent herbs to use, and should be freshly picked, before the plants flower. Pack them into a wide-mouthed jar, bruising slightly with a wooden spoon and pour on cider vinegar or white wine vinegar which has been brought just to boiling point. Cover tightly and leave in a warm place for 10 days, shaking the jar occasionally. Drain off the vinegar, put into clean bottles, and label carefully with the name of the herb. Use about 250 ml/½ pint herb leaves to each 500 ml/1 pint vinegar.

HERB JELLIES

Mint jelly is a traditional accompaniment for lamb, but delicious jellies may also be made with Parsley, Sage, Thyme and Bayleaves to accompany pork, ham and poultry. All herb jellies can easily be made from an apple jelly recipe, with a light colouring to make them particularly appetising.

Cut up 2.8 kg/6 lb apples in quarters, using the skins and cores as well, and chop 450 g/1 lb fresh Mint leaves. Cover with cold water, bring to the boil and simmer until the fruit is soft.

Leave in a jelly bag or clean tea towel to drip overnight and then measure the liquid. Allow 450 g/1 lb sugar to each pint/500 ml liquid and stir over gentle heat to dissolve sugar. Boil rapidly and test for setting on a cold saucer. When the jelly can be pushed with a finger and form wrinkles, it is ready for potting. Add a few drops of green vegetable colouring and some fresh mint leaves, chopped finely, and pour into small hot jars. Cover when cold.

Parsley, Sage and Thyme jelly can be made the same way. When potting Bayleaf jelly, do not add chopped leaves, but float a fresh leaf in each jar.

Flower Flavourings

The delicate scent of flowers can be given to fruit, preserves and cakes. The leaves of Cottage Geraniums, particularly the rose-scented variety, may be infused in apple jelly, or added to cooked apples, pears or blackberries. A leaf placed in the bottom of a sponge cake tin before the mixture is poured in and baked should be removed when the cake is turned out on a rack to cool and will leave the cake delicately flavoured. Lemon Verbena or Lemon Balm leaves may be used in the same way.

Lavender flowers and Rosemary leaves can be used to flavour fruit jellies, and they also make delicious sugar for flavouring cakes, biscuits and milk puddings. Make this sugar by putting sprigs of fresh Lavender or Rosemary into a screwtopped jar with castor sugar and leaving for at least 24 hours. Shake well and leave to stand again. Repeat the process for at least a week before using a little of the sugar for flavouring.

Marigold petals have been used for centuries, sprinkled on salads and cold meat dishes, and they can be infused in hot milk to give flavour and colour to cakes and custards. Nasturtium petals are also good as a garnish for both vegetables and fruit salads, or they can be chopped and added to cream cheese or butter, or lightly fried and added to chicken soup. Nasturtium leaves may also be chopped and used for salads and sandwiches.

Herb Butter

Pats of chilled herb-flavoured butter are a favourite accompaniment for steaks, chops and fish, or can be used on toast or in sandwiches.

Cream butter until soft and light and add a little lemon juice and plenty of chopped fresh herbs. These can be mixed, such as Parsley, Mint, Chives, Tarragon, and Marjoram (about 3 teaspoons herbs and 3 teaspoons lemon juice will flavour 100 g/4 oz butter), or a single herb such as Mint, Parsley or Chives can be used, according to the food. The herb butter is best left for 2 hours at room temperature so that the flavours mix and blend, and it can then be stored in a refrigerator or freezer.

HERB BREAD

Hot herb bread is a delicious accompaniment to savoury meals. Make this with a crusty French loaf and slash it through in 5 cm/2 in slices, not quite cutting to the bottom of the loaf. Spread herb butter between the slices and press the loaf back into shape. Wrap in foil and heat in a moderate oven for 20 minutes, then serve hot. Garlic or mixed herbs are favourite flavourings for bread. If garlic is used it should be lightly crushed with a knife before mixing with the butter.

HERB CHEESE

Flavoured cream cheese can be quickly prepared by mixing finely chopped fresh herbs (try Parsley, Thyme and Chives) with a crushed garlic clove, salt and pepper, and some cream cheese. It should be chilled before serving with biscuits or wholemeal bread.

Another delicious cheese is a mixture of grated Cheddar cheese with a little double cream, sherry, seasoning and chopped fresh herbs. Use 100 g/4 oz mixed herbs to 200 g/8 oz grated cheese, 2 tablespoons cream and 4 tablespoons dry sherry, and press the mixture into small pots before chilling. This mixture will keep for 5 days in a refrigerator if covered well.

HERB STUFFING

The secret of good stuffing is to make it light and crumbly with plenty of herbs which may be varied according to the food to be stuffed. The mixture should not contain much liquid or it will become heavy like a pudding when it absorbs the extra liquid from meat, poultry or fish. Thyme, Parsley and Marjoram are most useful stuffing herbs and a little lemon rind or juice will enhance their flavours.

WINTER MINT SAUCE

100 g/4 oz Mint leaves
100 g/4 oz sugar
250 ml/½ pint vinegar

Strip Mint leaves from stems and put them into a colander. Pour boiling water over them and then dry the leaves in a cloth. Sprinkle with 25 g/1 oz sugar and chop finely. Put the vinegar and remaining sugar into a saucepan and simmer for 3 minutes until the sugar has dissolved. Pack the Mint leaves into small jars and pour over the vinegar to cover the leaves. Seal with vinegar-proof lids. To use, dilute with a little more vinegar.

MOCK CAPERS

450 g/1 lb fresh Nasturtium seeds
500 ml/1 pint vinegar

25 g/1 oz salt
6 peppercorns

Gather the seeds on a dry day when they are young and soft, and wipe them clean. Put them into a dry jar and cover with the vinegar, salt and peppercorns. Cover tightly, and add a few more seeds from day to day if the jar is not full. Leave for a year before eating. They may be used instead of capers.

CANDIED ANGELICA

Fresh Angelica stems
7 g/¼ oz salt
2.2 l/4 pints water
Sugar

The Angelica stems should be used in April when they are tender. Cut the stems from the plant and cut into 7.5 cm/3 in pieces. Dissolve the salt in the water and bring to the boil. Pour this hot brine over the Angelica stems and leave for 10 minutes. Drain well and rinse in cold water. Put the stems into fresh boiling water and boil for 7 minutes until tender. Drain and scrape off the outer skin. Weigh the stems and take an equal weight of sugar.

Allow 500 ml/1 pint water for each 450 g/1 lb sugar. Dissolve the sugar in water, bring to the boil and pour over the stems. Leave for 24 hours.

Bring to the boil again and take out the stems. Take 450 g/1 lb sugar for each original 450 g/1 lb Angelica and add it to the syrup. Bring to the boil and pour over the stems. Leave for 24 hours, then repeat the process. Do this three

more times, and then leave the stems to soak in the syrup for 14 days. Drain very well, and put on a wire rack lined with greaseproof paper. Dry very slowly in a warm place such as an airing cupboard or over a cooker. Store in a covered jar. Use for cakes and for decoration.

CRYSTALLISED MINT LEAVES

Fresh Mint leaves
1 egg white
Granulated sugar

Use large, well-shaped, fresh green Mint leaves and wipe them dry very gently with kitchen paper. Beat the egg white to stiff peaks and coat both sides of each leaf. Dip the leaves into sugar until well covered, and put them on a wire rack covered with wax paper (use the lining paper from a cereal packet). Leave in a warm dry place until crisp. Store in an airtight container between layers of waxed paper. Use to garnish fruit dishes and ice cream.

MARIGOLD CONSERVE

450 g/15 oz Marigold petals
Lemon juice
450 g/1 lb sugar

Mash the petals with a wooden spoon, or use a blender on low speed. Add a little lemon juice to help the mashing process. Gradually work in the sugar until it is completely absorbed and put into small jars. Store in a cool place.

HERBS FOR HEALTH

Traditional herbal remedies handed down by countrywomen are based on well-known qualities of the ingredients. Some plants soothe, while others stimulate, and over the years the individual properties of herbs have been used to restore health and vigour, and to avoid small medical problems. Some herbs for instance reduce the effect of greasy food and encourage good digestion, so they were obviously used in recipes to prevent indigestion. Many herbs have been made into a form of tea, and according to the herb, these teas may soothe various organs, induce relaxation, or help to clear up skin troubles. Other herbs have soothing qualities when used externally, and are suitable for mixing with cream or oil to soothe sprains and strains, or to encourage healing. Herbal remedies are only supplementary to qualified medical advice and should not replace it, but they do help to avoid minor problems.

MEDICINAL HERB TEAS

Use fresh green or dried leaves for these infusions. Dried herbs are very strong in flavour, so use only one-third of the amount of fresh leaves, during the winter months. Three teaspoons fresh herbs will be enough for 1 large teacup of water. Put the leaves into a very clean teapot or covered jug and pour on boiling water. Leave to stand for 5 minutes before drinking. **Angelica** leaves stems, seeds and roots can be used for a tonic, which may be drunk hot once or twice a day, allowing up to 250 ml/½ pint a day.

Borage leaves and stems infused in boiling water and drunk before bed time help to promote sound sleep.

Camomile flowers in boiling water may be taken as a tonic, and are recommended to relieve insomnia, pain and soothe stomachs.

Comfrey is high in vitamins and minerals and the crushed roots simmered in water or milk make a tonic. The leaves may also be infused. Comfrey is reputed to heal wounds and soothe stomach ulcers, bowels, sore throats and chest infections.

Lemon Balm infused, makes a pleasant tonic, recommended to aid relaxation; to help reduce temperatures and sooth toothache and to improve the memory. A little lemon juice and sugar or honey will improve the flavour.

Marigold leaves or flower buds infused in boiling water will also help sound sleep, and the marigold tonic drunk during the day will help to improve the skin. It also has the reputation of helping to get rid of warts, strengthening a weak heart, eliminating varicose veins, ulcers, sickness, diarrhoea and toothache.

Pennyroyal leaves, flowers, stems and roots can all be infused and taken to soothe the nerves and lift depression, but it should not be taken when pregnant.

Peppermint leaves, flowers, stems and roots infused in water will aid digestion, calm the nerves and induce soothing sleep, and have the reputation of aiding those with migraine.

Rosemary flowers infused in boiling water should be cooled, strained and bottled. A wineglass of hot liquid will soothe headaches.

Yarrow leaves, stems and flowers can be infused to relieve colds and flu, and the infusion is reputed to correct diarrhoea and purify the blood.

TISANES

Infusions of aromatic culinary herbs are called *tisanes*, and are particularly popular in France to drink after meals or just before bedtime. These *tisanes* help to purify the blood and aid digestion, promote soothing sleep and calm the nerves. Fresh or dried herbs may be used, infused in boiling water and lightly sweetened with honey if liked. Mint, Sage, Lemon Balm, Marjoram, Thyme and Camomile are particularly delicious, and should be infused in earthenware, china or glass, as metal spoils the flavour. The leaves should not be left to soak too long in the water or the flavour will be ruined, and if a strong flavour is liked, it is better to use more herbs and infuse for a shorter-time. Usually 1 teaspoon dried herbs or 3 teaspoons fresh herbs will be enough for a cup of *tisane*, with just a little extra for a good flavour. Fresh herb leaves should be slightly bruised before infusing. Anise, Fennel and Caraway seeds may be infused if crushed slightly, allowing 1 tablespoon seeds to each 500 ml/pint of water.

SOOTHING INHALANTS

A heavy head cold can be lightened and soothed with a steaming inhalant, and one made from herbs is fragrantly pleasant. Use 4 tablespoons each of Peppermint leaves, Camomile leaves, Sage leaves and Lime flowers (lime flowers can be bought from a health food or herb shop). Put them in a bowl and pour on 1.1 litre/2 pints boiling water. Put the bowl on to a table at once and sit so that the head can easily be held over the steaming bowl. Put a towel over the head so that the steaming vapour does not escape and inhale for 15 minutes. Stay indoors for at least an hour afterwards, or go straight to bed. This 'steaming' is also very good for the complexion as it opens the pores and releases impurities.

SOOTHING OIL

This oil will help to soothe bruises and strains and can be made when the herbs are fresh and abundant, then stored for use. Mix together a large handful each of Lemon Balm, Rosemary and Sage leaves, Chamomile and Lavender flowers, and rosebuds, and chop them finely. Cover with salad oil and leave for 14 days, stirring frequently. After this time, heat the herbs gently in the oil until they become crisp and their herbal oils are extracted – the oil must not get hotter than boiling water. Strain through a piece of clean linen into a bottle or screwtop jar and keep tightly covered.

HERBS FOR BEAUTY

Many herbs have an indirect effect on beauty. Chewing Parsley, for instance, aids digestion and helps to promote a clear skin, as well as freshening the breath. Sage and Rosemary flavour foods, but also help to counteract the effect of fatty meats, and all kinds of herbal teas soothe the digestion, cleanse the skin and encourage relaxation. Attractive beauty aids can be prepared from herbs, which are far cheaper than commercial products and also make attractive gifts.

BATH SACHETS

A warm bath scented with herbs help to relax tired muscles, but nobody wants to relax in a sort of soup with herbs scattered around. The herbs are best put into small muslin or cheesecloth bags which can be infused in the warm water and then discarded, so a large supply is worth making. Make bath sachets the size of traditional lavender bags, and use a mixture of leaves from Mint, Thyme, Sage, Rosemary, Lemon Balm and Lemon Verbena with Lavender and Camomile flowers.

For a softening effect, use a mixture of medium oatmeal with mixed herbs. For each bag, use 2 tablespoons oatmeal to 1 tablespoon each of Rosemary, Camomile, crushed Bayleaves, Thyme and Basil. This oatmeal mixture can be used in two baths for economy, so keep a pretty saucer or bowl in the bathroom to hold the damp bag for second use.

BATH COLOGNE

Use a cheap eau-de-cologne for this, but add some special touches. Take a large breakfast-cup of very fragrant fresh rose petals and put them into a screwtop jar with a cup of cologne. Leave for 6 days, shaking occasionally. Mix together in a bowl 4 tablespoons finely grated lemon peel, 2 tablespoons freshly grated orange peel, 2 tablespoons fresh or dried Basil and 2 tablespoons fresh or dried Peppermint. Using the same large cup, measure 2 cups of boiling water and pour over the peels and herbs. Cover and leave to stand overnight. Strain the liquid into a clean screwtop jar and mix with the cologne drained from the rose petals. Shake well and keep tightly covered. Use as a scented body rub after a warm bath to freshen and invigorate the skin.

BATH ESSENCE

Those who like a liquid scent for the bath will like this refreshing mixture. Put 250 ml/½ pint water and 250 ml/½ pint cider vinegar into a saucepan and bring just to boiling point. Take off the heat and pour over 1 tablespoon dried Basil, 2 tablespoons dried Peppermint and 1 tablespoon Lemon Thyme. Cover and leave overnight. Strain liquid into a jar and keep stoppered. Add enough to the water to give a light scent.

SOOTHING FOOT BATH

Use this mixture to soak tired, sore feet. (Juniper berries can be bought at good chemists and grocers.)

Put into a large saucepan, 4 large handfuls each of Sage, Rosemary and Pennyroyal. Add 3 handfuls of Angelica leaves and 100 g/4 oz Juniper berries. Add 2.2 l/4 pts of water and bring to the boil. Simmer for 10 minutes and strain for use.

Plain Lavender in hot water also makes a refreshing foot bath.

HAIR TONICS

Rosemary is supposed to promote hair growth, and Sage is a tonic for the hair.

Put 4 tablespoons Rosemary or Sage leaves into a saucepan with 250 ml/½ pint cider vinegar and 250 ml/½ pint water. Bring to the boil and then simmer for 5 minutes. Cool, strain and bottle. Use a small pad of cotton wool to apply the lotion to the scalp daily.

Another Sage hair tonic is reputed to improve hair colour and tint away greyness: Put 1 tablespoon each of tea and dried Sage into a large jam jar and cover with boiling water. Put the jar into a saucepan of hot water and simmer over low heat for 2 hours. Cool, strain and bottle. Rub a little of this mixture into the scalp four or five times a week. This mixture will keep for a week, but 1 tablespoon eau-de-cologne may be added for longer keeping.

An oil-based tonic can be used to rub into the scalp before washing to improve the condition of the scalp: Put olive or almond oil into a screw-top jar and add a mixture of Sage, Thyme, Marjoram and Lemon Balm. Leave in a sunny place for a week before straining into a clean bottle. A similar mixture may be made by infusing Rosemary and Sage in cider vinegar in the same way.

TEETH WHITENER

A quick and simple whitener for the teeth is a rub with fresh Sage leaves.

Skin Cleanser

Boil 250 ml/½ pint water and add 3 tablespoons fresh Marigold petals. Simmer for 5 minutes and cool, strain and bottle. This will keep for a week and should be rubbed into the skin to act as a moisturiser, softener and tonic.

Eye Pads

Put a handful of Camomile flowers in a bowl and pour on a pint of boiling water. Leave to stand for 5 minutes. Wring out cotton wool pads in this infusion and put over closed eyes for 10 minutes.

Freckle Whitener

Warm a little clear honey and stir in some crushed Fennel seeds to make a thick mixture. Spread on the face like a mask and leave for 15 minutes. Wash off with warm water.

Shampoos

Camomile shampoos and rinses are good for fair hair, with Sage for dark hair. Rosemary helps to brighten and condition hair. Add these herbs to plain shampoos, or make up a mixture from soft soap and herbs to suit individual requirements.

HERBAL GIFTS

Herb leaves and flowers can be transformed into many delightful scented gifts for friends and for one's own home. Old-fashioned pot pourri, Lavender sticks and scented pillows are being revived because they scent the house and household linen deliciously, induce relaxation and help to keep away pests such as moths.

LAVENDER STICKS

These are sometimes known as Lavender bottles because of their shape, and were used to mark the dozens and half-dozens in grandmother's trousseau chest.

Pick the lavender when it is in full flower, but before it begins to drop, and cut long stems which are still supple. Take 18 or 22 heads, which will give an uneven number of pairs. Take a length of baby ribbon about 60 cm/2 ft long and tie the stems firmly together with one end of the ribbon immediately below the flower heads (**a**). Turn the bunch upside down and carefully bend the stalks out and down over the heads from the point where the ribbon is tied so that the heads look as if they are in a cage of stems (**b**). Space out the stalks in pairs evenly, and weave the long end of the ribbon over and under the stalks until the flower heads are com-pletely enclosed in a basketwork of ribbon (**c**). Make the weaving rather tight at the top and bottom of the heads and slacker in the centre to give the look of a bottle (**d**). When the heads are completely covered, wind the ribbon firmly round the stems in a spiral for an inch or two and then tie firmly in a bow (**e**). Leave about 3 ins. of stalk below the bow and trim to an even length with sharp scissors.

LINEN BAGS

Make small bags from muslin or light pretty fabric and fill with equal quantities of Rosemary leaves, Thyme and Bay leaves. Dry the herbs well and rub them small before using. Another fragrance can be obtained by using two parts of Mint, two parts of Rosemary and one part of Thyme with one part of ground cloves. Another scented linen bag can be made with a tablespoonful each of Lavender flowers, Rosemary leaves and Thyme with a teaspoon of Pennyroyal, crushed Cloves and dried lemon peel.

SCENTED PILLOWS

A scented pillow or cushion emits a delightful scent when lightly crushed and can be used to scatter on chairs, or to aid sleep in bedrooms. Make these little pillows from pretty silks, satins and laces, or crisply patterned cotton and stuff them with kapok in the usual way. Make small muslin bags of the selected herbs and tuck these into the cushions before they are closed – this gives a better texture to the pillow than loose herbs, and also makes it easier to wash the pretty cover. Try a teaspoon each of powdered dried Mint and ground cloves mixed with well-dried rose petals.

Another mixture consists of equal quantities of Lavender, Lemon Verbena leaves and Cottage Geranium leaves with a teaspoon each of dried lemon peel and powdered orris root. Orris root is obtainable from the chemist and is a fixative for scents.

POT POURRI

Bowls of pot pourri give a subtle scent to a room. The scent will be revived by gently stirring the bowl with the hand and putting the mixture in a warm place. Pot pourri used to be kept covered in jars like ginger jars, and the lid only taken off occasionally to release the scent which remains concentrated and strong. Today, pot pourri making has become a little more scientific and various fixatives and additives are available so that the pot pourri may be left in an open bowl and revived from time to time with essential oils or extra herbs and spices.

Pot pourri is a mixture of flowers, leaves and spices. All the herbs grown in a small space are suitable, mixed with spices which are in any kitchen cupboard. If few flowers are available, it is possible to make a mixture based on Lavender only, but many dried flower petals and leaves are obtainable from good chemists. Essential oils are also now widely available from chemists and from shops specialising in Eastern merchandise, and fixatives such as orris root and gum benzoin come either from the chemist or from shops specialising in herbal products.

Pick flowers and leaves in the peak of condition when they are not damp from rain or dew. Avoid thick fleshy flowers and only use the petals. Dry on wire cake racks, paper or muslin, in an airy dark place which is slightly warm. Bright light will fade colours, and too much warmth will dry out the fragrant oils. The flower petals are ready to use when they are crisp and rustle when moved, and the herb leaves should be brittle.

As the petals and leaves dry, put them in separate containers until there are enough to blend. Measure out the quantities required into a large biscuit tin or polythene box and mix well. Add spices and dry fixatives and then the fragrant oils drop by drop. Mix well and close up the box for six weeks, shaking occasionally to blend the ingredients. Put the pot pourri into pretty bowls around the house (it is worth looking for odd cups and bowls at jumble sales), and for gifts cover them with a little clingfilm to keep the mixture in place until delivered. Making pot pourri is rather like making cakes, and it is advisable to follow one or two basic detailed recipes before experimenting and introducing new ideas.

Lavender Pot Pourri

225 g/8 oz Lavender flowers
15 g/½ oz Thyme
15 g/½ oz Mint
25 g/1 oz cooking salt
8 g/¼ oz ground cloves
8 g/¼ oz ground Caraway seeds

Mix well together and put into a bowl. Use block cooking salt for this as free-running salt contains chemicals, and scrape the salt finely with a sharp knife.

Rose Pot Pourri

1 kg/2 lb red Rose petals
225 g/8 oz Lemon Verbena leaves
225 g/8 oz Cottage Geranium leaves
225 g/8 oz Lavender flowers
225 g/8 oz Rosemary leaves
15 g/½ oz Marjoram
15 g/½ oz Lemon Thyme
15 g/½ oz orris root powder
15 g/½ oz gum benzoin
15 g/½ oz ground allspice
15 g/½ oz ground cloves
Pinch of ground nutmeg
1 teaspoon dried orange peel
1 teaspoon dried lemon peel
10 drops Rose oil
3 drops Rosemary oil

Spread out the petals and leaves to dry, and store in separate containers. When all are dry and crisp, mix with the other ingredients and keep covered for six weeks, stirring occasionally. Put into bowls or jars.

SUPPLIERS

HERB PLANTS AND SEEDS

Daphne ffiske Herb Nursery, 2 Station New Road, Brundall, Norwich, Norfolk

Old Rectory Herb Farm, Ightham, near Sevenoaks, Kent

Stoke Lacy Herb Farm, Bromyard, Herefordshire

Yew Tree Herbs, Holt Street, Nonington, Near Dover, Kent

Tumblers Bottom Herb Farm, Kilmersdon, Radstock, Somerset

Lighthorne Herbs, Lighthorne Rouch, Moreton Morrell, Warwick

Suffolk Herbs, Sawyers Farm, Little Cornard, Sudbury, Suffolk

Chase Compost Seeds Ltd., Benhall, Saxmundham, Suffolk

Thompson & Morgan Ltd, Crane Hall, London Road, Ipswich, Suffolk

Dobie Seeds, Upper Dee Mills, Llangollen, Clwyd

A small selection of container-grown herbs can usually be found at garden centres, and in some health food shops. Everyday seeds such as Parsley can be found in ironmongers and other outlets where garden seeds are sold.

CONTAINERS, COMPOST AND TOOLS

A selection of containers, rooting and potting composts and tools may be foumd at garden centres, ironmongers, corn merchants, and general stores, and in large branches of some chemists.

AROMATIC OILS AND POT POURRI AIDS

(Mail Order)

Gerard House, 736b Christchurch Road, Boscombe, Bournemouth, Hants

Culpeper, Hadstock Road, Linton, Cambridge (also have shops in many cities)

Aromatic Oil Co., 131 Clapham High Street, London SW4 7SS

HERB GARDENS TO VISIT

Look up local opening times, or consult the National Trust Guide to Properties or the yellow book of The National Gardens Scheme, before visiting gardens.

Acorn Bank, Temple Sowerby, near Penrith, Cumbria (National Trust)

Hardwick Hall, Derbyshire (National Trust)

Felbrigg Hall, near Cromer, Norfolk (National Trust)

Sissinghurst Castle, Kent (National Trust)

Cranborne Manor Gardens, Wimborne, Dorset

Barnsley House Garden, near Cirencester, Glos.

Marndhill, Ardington, Berks

The Old Vicarage, Bucklebury, Berks

The Old Barn, Fremington, near Barnstaple, Devon

Holywell, Swanmore, Hants

Mawley Hall, Cleobury Mortimer, Salop

Stone Cottage, Hambleton, Leicestershire

Gaulden Manor, Tolland, Somerset

Coke's Cottage, West Burton, near Pulborough, Sussex

THE HERB SOCIETY

Those who become really interested in herbs and want to know more about growing and using them, and something of their fascinating history, might like to join The Herb Society, 34 Boscobel Place, London, SW1. Details of membership will be forwarded by the Secretary on receipt of a stamped addressed envelope.

Herbs and Their Uses

Herb	Culinary	Medical (inc. teas)	Beauty (inc. pot pourri)	Floral Arrangement
ANGELICA	*			
ANISE	*			
BALM	*	*	*	*
BASIL	*			
BAY	*		*	*
BORAGE	*			*
BURNET	*			
BERGAMOT	*	*	*	*
CAMOMILE		*	*	
CARAWAY	*			
CHERVIL	*			
CHIVES	*			
COMFREY	*	*		
CORIANDER	*			
COTTAGE GERANIUM	*		*	*
DANDELION	*			
DILL	*	*		
FENNEL	*			
GARLIC	*	*		
HYSSOP	*			*
LAVENDER	*		*	*
LEMON VERBENA			*	*
MARJORAM	*		*	
MINT	*		*	
NASTURTIUM	*			*
PENNYROYAL	*	*		
PARSLEY	*			
POT MARIGOLD	*	*		*
PURSLANE	*			
ROSEMARY	*		*	*
SAGE	*	*		*
SAVORY	*			
SORREL	*			
TARRAGON	*			
THYME	*		*	*
YARROW				*

THE HERBAL CALENDAR

A GUIDE TO THE AVAILABILITY OF FRESH HERBS

SPRING

Angelica
Bay
Burnet
Camomile
Comfrey
Cottage Geranium
Dandelion
Hyssop
Rosemary
Sage
Thyme

SUMMER

Anise (leaves)
Borage
Balm
Basil
Bay
Burnet
Bergamot
Chives
Caraway (leaves)
Coriander (leaves)
Comfrey
Camomile
Chervil
Cottage Geranium
Dandelion
Dill
Fennel
Hyssop
Lavender
Lemon Verbena
Marjoram
Mint
Nasturtium
Parsley
Pennyroyal
Purslane
Pot Marigold
Rosemary
Sage
Sorrel
Summer Savory
Thyme
Tarragon
Yarrow

AUTUMN

Anise (seeds)
Balm
Bay
Burnet
Caraway (seeds)
Coriander (seeds)
Comfrey
Camomile
Cottage Geranium
Garlic
Hyssop
Lavender
Marjoram
Mint
Parsley
Rosemary
Sage
Thyme
Winter Savory

WINTER

Bay
Cottage Geraniums
Hyssop
Rosemary
Sage
Thyme
Winter Savory

GARDEN CALENDAR

Herb	Sowing or Planting	Sun or Shade	Harvesting	Special Cultivation
ANGELICA	Spring	Half-shade	April/May	Keep fairly damp and well fed
ANISE	April	Full sun	Autumn	Needs very warm weather to ripen seed
BALM	Spring	Sun	Summer	Allow plenty of space in large container
BASIL	Spring	Full sun	Summer	Likes dry, rich soil and shelter
BAY	Spring	Sun	Year round	Well-drained soil and shelter. Beware of frost. Will grow very large after some years
BERGAMOT	March	Sun	Summer	Likes wet, rich soil
BORAGE	Spring	Sun	Summer	Light, well-drained soil
BURNET	Spring or Autumn	Sun	Spring/Autumn	Does best in chalk
CAMOMILE	Spring or Autumn	Sun	Summer	Dryish, sandy soil
CARAWAY	Late Summer or Spring	Sun	Autumn	Dry soil preferred
CHERVIL	Spring	Half-shade	Summer	Light, moist soil
CHIVES	Spring	Shade	Summer	Rich, wet soil
COMFREY	Any time	Sun	Summer	Transplants easily
CORIANDER	Spring	Sun	Autumn	Ordinary soil
COTTAGE GERANIUMS	Any time	Sun	Any time	Excellent house plants
DANDELION	Spring	Sun	Spring/Summer	Blanch leaves under pots for crispness
DILL	Spring	Sun	Summer	Dryish, ordinary soil
FENNEL	Spring	Sun	Summer	Well-drained soil
GARLIC	Spring	Full sun	Autumn	Rich, well-drained soil
HYSSOP	Spring	Sun	Any time	Well-drained soil. Trim shape in autumn
LAVENDER	Autumn	Full sun	Summer	Well-drained soil with lime. Clip into shape in autumn or spring
LEMON VERBENA	Spring	Full sun	Summer	Dry, not too rich soil. Trim into neat shape
MARJORAM	Spring	Full sun	Summer	Well-drained, not too dry soil. Cut regularly to encourage growth

Herb	Sowing or Planting	Sun or Shade	Harvesting	Special Cultivation
MINT	Spring	Sun or Half-shade	Summer	Wet ordinary soil
NASTURTIUM	Spring	Sun	Summer	Not too rich soil.
PARSLEY	Spring	Half-shade	Summer	Moist but well-drained soil, with some lime. Slow to germinate
PENNYROYAL	Spring	Half-shade	Summer	Damp sheltered site
POT MARIGOLD	Spring	Sun	Summer	Happy in any soil
PURSLANE	Spring	Sun	Summer	Likes hot dry soil Sow monthly for good supplies
ROSEMARY	Spring	Full sun	Summer	Sandy, well-drained soil. Keep protected in winter, and protect from wet roots

Herb	Sowing or Planting	Sun or Shade	Harvesting	Special Cultivation
SAGE	Spring	Full sun	Summer	Dry ordinary soil, as hates wet winter conditions. Trim to keep in shape
SAVORY (SUMMER & WINTER)	Spring	Full sun	Summer/ Winter	Ordinary soil Germinates slowly
SORREL	Spring	Sun or Half-shade	Summer	Light, moist and fairly rich soil
TARRAGON	Spring or Autumn	Full sun	Summer	Dry, good soil. Protect from frost, and do not cut down old growth until Spring
THYME	Spring	Full sun	Summer	Dry, ordinary soil, keep well trimmed
YARROW	Spring	Sun or Half-shade	Summer	Will grow anywhere

INDEX